PERSONAL SECURITY DATA IN AN INCREASINGLY DIGITAL WORLD

PERSONAL SECURITY DATA IN AN INCREASINGLY DIGITAL WORLD

Authors:

Austin Mardon

Muhammad Ans

Suhaib Aldada

Sapna Rameshwarsingh

Julia Cara

Jessica Henschel

David Henneberg

Mya George

Michael Phan

Abeer Ansari

Alicia Au

Ryan Doleweerd

Christina Nguyen

Hala Mahdi

Editor:
Catherine Mardon

Published by Golden Meteorite Press

Golden Meteorite Press

103 11919 82 St NW

Edmonton, AB T5B 2W3

www.goldenmeteoritepress.com

ISBN: 978-1-77369-906-6

EBook ISBN: 978-1-77369-907-3

GM

PRESS

Typeset and Cover Design by Nadia Feller

Table of Contents

INTRODUCTION

Data privacy is the protection of personal information from unauthorized access or use. It is a crucial part of data security, which guards data from unauthorized access, use, modification, or destruction. The increasing amount of personal data stored and shared online has made data privacy a more pressing issue. To protect personal information, it is essential to understand data privacy and the various stakeholders involved, including individuals, organizations, governments, and technology companies. Data privacy can be safeguarded through effective policies and procedures that ensure the privacy and security of data. Organizations must also ensure that their data privacy policies follow applicable laws.

Later on, this book focuses on what privacy, anonymity and security can entail and how they can be properly assessed. There will also be general information surrounding these topics that will better inform the reader on how to protect themselves online. To keep your personal data secure online, it is recommended to use strong and complex passwords, avoid public Wi-Fi networks, enable two-factor authentication, and be aware of phishing schemes. It is also important to keep your software and operating system up to date, use a secure web browser, and be cautious about the websites you visit and the information you share. By following these best practices, you can help protect yourself against security risks on the internet. Later on, data breaches within 2 companies are examined. The timelines and ripple effects of Facebook and Amazon show how common and easily it can happen. This examination is in hopes of highlighting the need of policies to be put in place to prevent further data breaches in the future.

Algorithmic accountability is a relatively new area of concern in discussions about the ethics of artificial intelligence's practical uses. How do individuals understand, work under, and contest any decisions made by a machine rather than a human? Who is ultimately responsible if harm is incurred by algorithms' choices? In this short primer section, the North American context of algorithmic accountability is explored. The use of facial recognition technologies (FRTs) continues to take our world by storm. The promise is that these technologies will make our lives easier. However, FRTs appear to be a double-edged sword because they possess as many risks, if not more, than their perceived benefits. This book analyzes the recent developments in FRTs and the role of the social media giant META in using facial recognition technologies.

Have you ever scanned your fingerprint to unlock your phone? Or use face recognition to open your apps? This type of security is known as smartphone biometrics which uses unique physiological and behavioural traits to identify and verify individuals. There are many types of biometric data such as face recognition, fingerprint scanning, gait-based authentication, and iris recognition. These types of data along with the background and future directions of biometrics are discussed in this chapter.

Identity verification for travel purposes has historically relied on cross referencing one's physical identification, particularly their passport, with their appearance in-person. Placing trust in one's physical documentation and the ability of airport staff to judge whether one is being truthful and if their identity is correct makes the aviation industry weak to abuses. Integrating biometric screening, coming to rely on stronger points of identification such as screening fingerprints and utilizing facial recognition, into airport security has the ability to strengthen identification efforts and to increase overall efficiency within travel. A later chapter in this book focuses on the Closed Circuit Television System (CCTV). It will briefly describe the history and evolution of CCTV surveillance from the very first of its kind technology to how it is currently being used. The chapter also dives into the pros and cons of using CCTV surveillance as well the future of surveillance through artificial intelligence.

There is also a chapter dedicated to the discussion of smart home technology. Specifically, how this technology has the goal to improve the comfort and lifestyle of the smart home tenant. This smart home technology has many different possible appliances, from applications both to improve the comfort, but also improves the home security. Some of the new smart appliances do pose risks to privacy such as smart personal assistants. In today's day and age, the Internet is a tool utilised worldwide more than ever before. As such, it has also never been easier and more convenient for the search engines and social media applications so commonly used to collect user data and profit from it. This chapter will serve as an overview of the types of data collected and the methods of data collection used by these entities, the general user perspective on personal data privacy, privacy-led alternative search engines, and some possibly overlooked beneficial applications of the data collected.

WHAT IS DATA PRIVACY?

By Suhaib Aldada

Introduction

Data privacy is the practice of protecting data from unauthorized use, access, or disclosure. It is an essential part of data security, which protects data from unauthorized access, use, modification, or destruction. Data privacy is essential for protecting personal information in the digital age. In recent years, data privacy has become a more pressing issue as more and more information is stored and shared online. With the rapid development of technology, the amount of data collected, stored, and shared has grown exponentially. As a result, the need to protect this data and ensure its privacy has become increasingly important. Data privacy is a complex issue that involves multiple stakeholders, including individuals, organizations, governments, and technology companies (Petters, 2020). Understanding the different aspects of data privacy is essential to protect personal information. This essay will explore the concept of data privacy and discuss its importance in the modern world. It will also examine the various stakeholders involved in data privacy and how it can be protected. Data privacy is the practice of ensuring the security of personal information and preventing unauthorized access or use of this data. This can be achieved through effective policies and procedures that ensure the privacy and security of data. Organizations must ensure that their data privacy policies are up to date and comply with applicable laws.

Additionally, individuals must be aware of their rights and how their data can be protected. Data privacy has become a significant issue in the digital age due to the increasing amount of data collected, stored, and shared online. This data can include sensitive information such as credit card numbers, personal addresses, and medical records. As such, it is essential that this data is protected and that its privacy is maintained. Data privacy is also essential for governments, technology companies, and other organizations. Governments must make sure that the information in collection is stored and secured and not used for unauthorized purposes. Technology companies have to make sure the data in collection and storage is secured and not used for unauthorized purposes.

Additionally, organizations must ensure that their data privacy policies are up to date and comply with applicable laws. Data privacy is an important issue that must be taken seriously to protect personal information in the digital age. It is essential for individuals, organizations, governments, and technology companies to understand the different aspects of data privacy and how it can be protected. By understanding data privacy and taking the necessary steps to protect it, individuals, organizations, and governments can ensure the security of their data and the privacy of their information (SNIA, 2021). Data privacy is an increasingly relevant and vital topic today, as it is essential for protecting the personal information of individuals, as well as safeguarding businesses and organizations from cyber threats. This essay will explore the concept of data privacy, its implications, and its importance in the digital age.

History of Data Privacy

Evolution of Data Privacy

Data privacy is a concept that has been evolving for centuries. It is a complex issue that has been addressed in different ways throughout history. In the past, data privacy was addressed primarily through the physical protection of personal information, such as keeping documents in locked cabinets, encrypting data, and other methods. With the emergence of the digital age, however, data privacy has become even more complex and essential (HubSpot, 2022).

The evolution of data privacy has been driven by the development of technology that has made it easier to collect, store, process, and personal access data. As data collection and storage have become ubiquitous, concerns over the security and privacy of that data have grown. In response to these concerns, governments worldwide have implemented laws and regulations to protect the privacy of individuals (HubSpot, 2022).

One of the first significant laws in the United States was the Health Insurance Portability and Accountability Act of 1996 (HIPAA). This law was designed to protect healthcare information's privacy and ensure the data's security. Since then, numerous other laws have been passed to protect personal data privacy, which includes the Gramm-Leach-Bliley Act, the Children's Online Privacy Protection Act, and the California Consumer Privacy Act. These laws have been developed to address the complexities of data privacy in the digital age. For example, the California Consumer Privacy Act has been designed to ensure that companies are transparent about the types of data they collect and how they use it. This includes the right for consumers to access, delete, and opt out of certain types of data collection. In addition to laws, other measures have been taken to protect personal data privacy. One of the most important is encryption, which is data scrambling so those with the correct encryption key can only access it. Encryption protects data stored on computers, in the cloud, and other places (Compliance, 2021).

In recent years, the development of artificial intelligence (AI) has raised additional concerns about data privacy. AI technologies are being used to analyze large amounts of data, often without the knowledge or consent of the individuals whose data is being used. To address these concerns, governments are beginning to implement laws and regulations specifically targeting the use of AI for data collection and processing. As technology continues to evolve, so will the issue of data privacy. New laws, regulations, and other measures will be needed to ensure that personal data is protected and that individuals have control over how their data is used. It is essential for individuals to be aware of their rights and to understand the laws that protect them. Only by staying informed and aware can individuals ensure that their data privacy is protected (Compliance, 2021).

Data Privacy in the Digital Age

Data privacy is an increasingly important issue in the digital age. With the advancement of technology, more and more data are being collected, stored, and shared. As this data can be used to track individuals and make decisions about them, it is essential to protect the privacy of individuals and ensure that their data is not abused. Data privacy is the right of an individual to be in control of their private data. This includes the right to decide when, how, and to whom their data is shared. Data privacy also includes the right to be informed of how their information is being used and to have the ability to make changes or opt out of how the data is used (Altshuler, 2019).

Data privacy is paramount in the digital age as more and more data are being collected, stored, and shared. This data can be used to track individuals and make decisions about them, such as their credit score or whether they are eligible for a job. Therefore, it is essential to protect individuals' data and ensure that it is not used for malicious or exploitative purposes. In order to protect data privacy, organizations must implement appropriate measures to ensure that data is securely stored and only used for legitimate purposes. This includes implementing strong security measures, such as encryption and authentication, to protect data from unauthorized access. It also includes implementing data access and usage policies that specify who can access the data, how it can be used, and what processes must be followed when accessing or using it.

Organizations must also ensure that individuals are informed of how their data is being used and that they can make changes or opt-out of how it is used. Individuals must also be able to access and update their data to ensure that it is accurate and up-to-date. Finally, organizations must be transparent in how they use data and be willing to answer any questions individuals may have. This includes informing individuals of any data-sharing practices and allowing them to opt out of any data-sharing. Data privacy is essential in the digital age, and organizations must take appropriate measures to protect individuals' data. By implementing strong security measures, data access and usage policies, informing individuals of how their data is being used, and being transparent in how data is used, organizations can help ensure that individuals' data is not abused (Nations, 2021).

Data privacy is becoming increasingly important in the modern world. With the widespread use of the Internet, people's data is more accessible than ever. Companies, governments, and even criminals can access and utilize this data. As such, individuals need to protect their data and ensure their privacy is respected. Having strong data privacy practices helps protect people from identity theft, data breaches, and other malicious activities. It also helps protect one's freedom of expression, as people can feel more comfortable sharing their thoughts and opinions without fear of misusing their data. Data privacy laws also help to protect people's privacy by setting clear rules on how companies should handle personal data. Overall, data privacy is an important issue that needs to be taken seriously in the modern world. Individuals need to understand their rights regarding their data and ensure that their privacy is respected. It is also essential for companies and governments to ensure that they are compliant with data privacy laws and respect the privacy of their customers and citizens (Nations, 2021).

Benefits of Data Privacy

Increased security

Data privacy is an important and necessary measure to protect consumer data and personal information. Increased security is one of the critical benefits that data privacy offers. By limiting and controlling access to sensitive data, organizations can reduce the risk of a security breach and protect their customers' information. Enhanced security measures such as encryption, access control, and user authentication can help protect data from unauthorized access while providing an extra layer of protection against malicious actors attempting to gain access to confidential information. Additionally, data privacy can help organizations ensure that their customer's data is used responsibly and assist in meeting various compliance regulations (ico, 2022).

Protection of personal information

Data privacy is an important consideration when it comes to protecting personal information. By protecting personal information, individuals can be assured that their data will be kept secure, confidential, and only used for the purposes for which it was intended. Companies must ensure that their data processing and storage systems are secure and follow accepted security protocols (Bank, 2021).

One of the main benefits of data privacy is protecting personal information. This means that individuals can choose how their data is used and shared, and companies must respect their wishes. Companies must also ensure that their data is stored securely and not shared with third parties without the individual's consent. Additionally, data privacy laws require companies to inform individuals of how their data is being collected and used.

Data privacy also helps to protect individuals from identity theft, fraud, and other malicious activities. By protecting individuals' personal information, companies can help reduce the risk of such activities occurring. Data privacy also helps prevent data breaches, which can have severe consequences for individuals and companies (Bank, 2021).

Data privacy gives individuals a sense of security and control over their personal information. By understanding the benefits of data privacy and implementing the necessary safeguards, companies and individuals can ensure that their data is kept secure and confidential (Bank, 2021).

Improved trust in online services

Data privacy is a critical factor for ensuring trust in online services. By respecting user privacy, companies can build trust with their customers and protect their data from unauthorized access. By controlling access to personal data, companies can ensure that users are comfortable providing information on their services. This trust can increase customer satisfaction, as users know their data is safe and secure. Additionally, by putting in place measures to protect user data, companies can prevent data breaches, thus reducing the potential for identity theft, fraud, and other cybercrimes. Finally, improved trust in online services can lead to better customer relationships and loyalty, resulting in increased sales and customer retention (Bank, 2021).

Challenges of Data Privacy

Lack of universal regulations

Data privacy remains a significant challenge for businesses and organizations. Although data privacy regulations exist in many countries, there is no universal regulation governing data privacy. This lack of universal regulations presents several challenges.

First, businesses and organizations must comply with multiple and often conflicting data privacy regulations. This can be costly and time-consuming, as organizations must keep track of different regulations in multiple countries. Furthermore, the need for a unified approach to data privacy means that organizations may have to choose which regulations to comply with and may be forced to sacrifice data privacy in one jurisdiction to comply with regulations in another (CloverDX, 2020).

Second, the need for a unified approach means inconsistent data privacy regulations. This can create confusion for organizations, as well as confusion for users. For example, a user may be asked to consent to data collection practices in one country that would be illegal in another, or a user may be asked to give consent to data collection practices that are not allowed in the same country.

Finally, the lack of universal regulations means that the en-

forcement of data privacy regulations could be more asser-
tive. This can create an environment in which organizations
are not held accountable for data privacy breaches, which can
severely damage users and organizations (CloverDX, 2020).

The lack of universal regulations presents a significant challenge to data privacy. Organizations must comply with multiple and often conflicting regulations, while users must navigate a confusing and inconsistent landscape. Furthermore,
the lack of enforcement can create an environment where
data privacy breaches are not taken seriously.

Difficulty of enforcement

Enforcement of data privacy regulations can be a difficult
challenge for companies to undertake. With the vast amounts
of data collected, stored, and shared on a global scale, companies must have the resources and technology to track,
monitor, and audit data usage. This requires companies to be
aware of the scope of data they have collected and stored,
and where it is located, which can be difficult and time-consuming. Furthermore, these regulations can often be complex
and difficult to interpret, making it challenging to identify and
punish violators. These challenges can be compounded by
the need for companies to invest in data privacy enforcement,
which can be costly and time-consuming. In order for companies to effectively enforce data privacy regulations, they must
have access to the resources and technology necessary to
track, monitor, and audit usage. This includes understanding
the data they have collected and stored, and where it is located, as well as being able to interpret complex and challenging regulations. Additionally, companies must be motivated
to invest in data privacy enforcement, as it can be costly and
time-consuming. To do this, companies may need to have access to legal resources, technology, and personnel dedicated
to enforcing data privacy regulations. Overall, enforcement of

data privacy regulations can be a challenging task for companies to undertake. To effectively do so, they must possess the resources and technology to track, monitor, and audit usage, as well as being able to interpret and identify violations. This can be compounded by the need for companies to invest in data privacy enforcement, which can be costly and time-consuming. However, with the correct resources and personnel, companies can ultimately be successful in enforcing data privacy regulations.

Issues with data breaches

Data breaches can occur when unauthorized people access personal data. This can occur due to weak security measures, hacking, or malicious intent. Unauthorized access can lead to identity theft and other financial losses (DataGrail, 2022).

Data breaches can lead to a loss of trust in an organization. Customers may feel that their personal information has been compromised and may no longer trust the business. In some cases, customers may even take their business elsewhere, leading to financial loss.

Data breaches can lead to financial and legal liability for the organization. Depending on the country's laws, organizations may be held responsible for any losses due to a data breach (DataGrail, 2022).

Data breaches can damage an organization's reputation, as customers may no longer trust or be willing to do business with them. This can lead to declining sales, profits, and stock prices. Depending on the country's laws, organizations may face hefty fines from regulatory bodies for data breaches. This can be costly and result in long-term financial losses (Data-Grail, 2022).

Data breaches can lead to data leakage, where confidential information is mistakenly or maliciously released to third parties. This can lead to financial losses, as well as a loss of trust from customers (DataGrail, 2022).

Conclusion

Data privacy protects private data, like names, addresses, Social Security numbers, credit card numbers, and other sensitive information, from unauthorized access or use. It involves the collections, storage, uses, and disposal of private data in a secure way. Data privacy laws and regulations exist in many countries to protect individuals' data and ensure that organizations are responsible for handling sensitive data. Data privacy is an essential concept in an increasingly digital world, and organizations have to give protection to the data of their customers, employees, and partners. Data privacy is becoming increasingly important in the modern world. With the widespread use of the Internet, people's data is more accessible than ever. Companies, governments, and even criminals can access and utilize this data. As such, individuals need to protect their data and ensure their privacy is respected. Having strong data privacy practices helps protect people from identity theft, data breaches, and other malicious activities. It also helps protect one's freedom of expression, as people can feel more comfortable sharing their thoughts and opinions without fear of misusing their data. Data privacy laws also help to protect people's privacy by setting clear rules on how companies should handle personal data. Overall, data privacy is an important issue that needs to be taken seriously in the modern world. Individuals need to understand their rights regarding their data and ensure that their privacy is respected. It is also essential for companies and governments to ensure that they are compliant with data privacy laws and respect the privacy of their customers and citizens.

References

Altshuler, T. (2019, September 26). Privacy in a digital world. TechCrunch. https://techcrunch.com/2019/09/26/privacy-queen-of-human-rights-in-a-digital-world/

Bank, W. (2021, September 21). Data protection and privacy laws | Identification for Development. Id4d.worldbank.org. https://id4d.worldbank.org/guide/data-protection-and-privacy-laws

Cawthon, P. (2022, July 15). Top Data Privacy Issues: Examples and Solutions. Incognito. https://incogniton.com/top-data-privacy-issues/

CloverDX. (2020, January). The 8 Most Challenging Data Privacy Issues (and How to Solve Them). Www.cloverdx.com. https://www.cloverdx.com/blog/data-privacy-issues-and-how-to-solve-them

Compliance, P. (2021, August 21). Evolution of Data Privacy. Planet Compliance. https://www.planetcompliance.com/evolution-of-data-privacy/

Cott, J. V. (2020, January 9). Key Data Privacy Issues and Trends for 2020. Lepide Blog: A Guide to IT Security, Compliance and IT Operations. https://www.lepide.com/blog/key-data-privacy-issues-and-trends-for-2020/

DataGrail. (2022, May 4). 6 Common Data Privacy Issues. DataGrail. https://www.datagrail.io/blog/data-privacy/data-privacy-issues/#:~:text=Malicious%20third%20parties%20may%20infiltrate

Didomi. (2022, January 14). Benefits of complying with data privacy laws | Didomi. Blog.didomi.io. https://blog.didomi.io/en-us/benefits-data-privacy-laws

Emotiv. (2019, January 21). What is Data Privacy? Definition & FAQs. EMOTIV. https://www.emotiv.com/glossary/data-privacy/

HubSpot. (2022, January 28). Reflections on the Evolution of Data Privacy. Medium. https://medium.com/@HubSpot/reflections-on-the-evolution-of-data-privacy-754bc31f3809

IAPP. (2018). What is Privacy. Iapp.org. https://iapp.org/about/what-is-privacy/

ico. (2022, June 8). The benefits of data protection laws. Ico.org.uk. https://ico.org.uk/for-organisations/sme-web-hub/the-benefits-of-data-protection-laws/#:~:text=As%20well%20as%20being%20the

Karlsgate. (2021). History of Privacy Timeline / safecomputing.umich.edu. Safecomputing.umich.edu. https://safecomputing.umich.edu/privacy/history-of-privacy-timeline

Manager, D. P. (2020, August 20). 5 things you need to know about Data Privacy. Data Privacy Manager. https://dataprivacymanager.net/5-things-you-need-to-know-about-data-privacy/

Nations, U. (2021, December 21). OHCHR | OHCHR and privacy in the digital age. OHCHR. https://www.ohchr.org/en/privacy-in-the-digital-age

Panel®, E. (2022, May 21). Council Post: 16 Effective Ways Business Can Build Trust Online. Forbes. https://www.forbes.com/sites/forbescoachescouncil/2020/07/20/16-effective-ways-business-can-build-trust-online/?sh=3c50fbe9632f

Petters, J. (2020, September 28). Data Privacy Guide: Definitions, Explanations and Legislation. Www.varonis.com. https://www.varonis.com/blog/data-privacy

SONIA. (2021, September 21). What is Data Privacy? | SNIA. Www.snia.org. https://www.snia.org/education/ what-is-data-privacy

Talend. (2021, November 26). What is Data Privacy? Definition and Compliance Guide. Talend Real-Time Open Source Data Integration Software. https://www.talend. com/resources/data-privacy/

UN, I. (2022, July 24). Three Challenges in Data Protection and Privacy | IOM Blog. Weblog.iom.int. https://weblog. iom.int/three-challenges-data-protection-and-privacy

WHAT IS PERSONAL SECURITY DATA?

By Julia Cara

Introduction

There is no debate: for better or worse, we find ourselves living increasingly digital lives. From TV show streaming and social media to online banking, online shopping, and online dating – we are able to use the internet to fulfill nearly every want or need imaginable. In many ways these technological advances have been convenient tools to enhance our lives and facilitate our daily chores and activities. During the Covid-19 pandemic, it enabled us to work and go to school remotely, arrange contactless grocery deliveries, and communicate public health information amongst our isolated population. Social media entertained us, taught us new skills, and kept us connected to one another. The internet was, by many accounts, a lifesaver. However, the rise of this hyper-digital age brings with it a new set of dangers – among them, the growing threat of online exploitation.

Over the past few decades, the issue of personal data and privacy has slowly come to the forefront of public consciousness as our online interactions have become more commonplace. It is important to note that we divulge personal information online all the time. Whether you are signing up for a social media platform, ordering food, entering a contest, or buying something online, you are likely sharing more personally identifiable data than you are aware of. At the least: your name, age, email, and phone number. But also frequently: credit card numbers, personal addresses, and demographic and behavioural information.

This information, should it fall into the wrong hands, can be used for exploitative purposes. Thus, it has become increasingly important for individuals to be aware of their rights when it comes to their personal security data and privacy. In this chapter, we will define personal security data, explore the current state of privacy laws in Canada, and discuss the trade and misuse of sensitive personal information.

Personal Security Data: Definitions and Canadian Laws

Personal security data, or personally identifiable information (PII), is any information that can be used to identify an individual and compromise their safety or security. According to the American Computer Security Resource Center, personally identifiable information is defined as "any information about an individual maintained by an agency" which can be "used to distinguish or trace an individual's identity" (CSRC). This also includes any data that is "linked or linkable to an individual, such as medical, educational, financial, and employment information" (CSRC).

Many pieces of information fall into these categories, including a person's full name, home address, phone number, date of birth, or social insurance number. Personal security data can also include information about one's race, religion, age, marital status, medical history, or genetics and DNA.

Information can be considered 'personal' if it directly identifies someone, or if it can be combined with another piece of data to identify an individual. For example, a social insurance number (SIN) by itself doesn't necessarily identify someone. However, combined with a name or birthdate, that SIN becomes an identifiable piece of information. Similarly, information about a person's habits, routines, and personal relationships – although not typically considered 'sensitive' – can also be considered personal security data if it can be used to track someone or create a profile about their behaviours. It is important to keep this data protected and secure to prevent identity theft, fraud, and other crimes.

In Canada, this data is protected under Canadian privacy laws. The two major federal privacy laws are the Privacy Act, and the Personal Information Protection and Electronic Documents Act better known as PIPEDA (Privacy Commissioner). Together, these laws regulate how the federal government and business organizations handle the collection and storage of personal information. This includes requirements for obtaining consent, protecting personal data from unauthorized access or disclosure by unrelated parties, and providing individuals with access to their own personal data upon request. PIPEDA also provides individuals the right to complain to the Office of the Privacy Commissioner of Canada if they believe their personal data has been misused or abused by an organization. Similarly, the Privacy Act protects a person's right to access and correct any personal information that the Government of Canada has on record about them. PIPEDA does not always apply in Alberta, British Columbia, or Québec, however these provinces have provincial privacy laws that govern organizations in a similar manner (Privacy Commissioner). Additionally, some provinces have privacy laws related to health information, like the Ontario Personal Health Information Protection Act. Health laws balance protecting the privacy and confidentiality of a patient while still facilitating the access to and dissemination of health care.

All of these laws require private-sector organizations and federally regulated businesses to take precautionary steps to ensure the security and confidentiality of the personal information they collect (Privacy Commissioner).

International Laws

The issue of privacy and data protection an international one, and has become increasingly recognized worldwide. However, there are no legal instruments or policies that govern data protection on an international scale. Instead, privacy laws are governed on a national, regional, or territorial level.

According to the United Nations Conference on Trade and Development, 137 of 194 countries have signed legislation governing the collection and protection of sensitive personal data (UNCTAD). These international laws generally fall under three categories: data protection privacy laws, cybercrime laws, and consumer protection laws. However, at least 15% of the world's countries still have no laws related to this issue (UNCTAD).

The United States employs several legal policies. The Children's Online Privacy Protection Act (COPPA), protects the privacy of children 13 and under by prohibiting the collection of their personal data (Clinen). As children are one of the most vulnerable groups online and offline, these laws are one essential tool to protect them as they learn to navigate the digital world. Many organizations understand the potential risks to children on social media sites – from risky TikTok trends to predatory adults asking for sensitive information – and many platforms have age requirements for these reasons.

The European Union created the General Data Protection Regulation (GDPR) which came into effect in 2018 (Cline). This law gives European Union citizens more control over what information they have to share online, and how that information is used. Users can request to view their data and have it deleted. Businesses must also "obtain clear, explicit consent" in order to use personal data for marketing or to share it with third parties (Clinen). Further, it requires that businesses notify authorities of data breaches within 72 hours of a breach (Clinen). Interestingly, the GDPR differentiates 'general personal data' and 'sensitive personal data'. 'Sensitive personal data' is subject to higher levels of protection and includes: genetic, biometric and health-related data; data that reveals one's racial or ethnic origin, political opinions, religious or ideological convictions; data pertaining to trade union membership; and data which concerns details about a person's sex life or sexual orientation (European Commission).

When is Data No Longer Considered 'Personally Identifiable'?

For data to cease to be personally identifiable, it must be anonymized in such way that no single individual can be identified from the data. Further, this anonymization must be irreversible. Encrypted data is still personally identifiable as the information can be unencrypted and used to re-identify a person (European Commission).

The Trade of Personal Data and Privacy Economics

With the rise of the internet came advancements in information technology which "vastly enlarged the amount of individual information that can be collected, stored, analyzed, and repurposed for new uses" (Acquisti). Instead of companies keeping filing cabinets full of paper records of their customers, hundreds of thousands of data points can be stored in a single Excel sheet or online database. Not only does this mean that more information is being collected and stored for longer, but this data is increasingly being traded, shared, and used without the knowing consent of the individuals who supply it. As one expert states, consumers often have "imperfect information regarding when their data is collected, with what purposes, and with what consequences" (Acquisti).

Consider the last time you signed up for a social media site or had to make an account to access information on a website. You likely entered personal information including your full name, age, email, address and postal code. Perhaps you were also asked questions about your occupation, education, or interests. Perhaps an app requested access to your contacts, or to be linked to your Facebook account. All of these pieces of information, and links to your other online presences, begins to build a profile of who you are as a person and what interests you. The old adage of 'knowledge is power' is true, and as such these data profiles have inherent value on the market. If a company understands your spending habits, for example, they can create more effective marketing directed at you.

Privacy economics is a branch of economics that studies the value of personal data and the trade-offs that both individuals and organizations make in relation to their privacy. This can include things like the cost of collecting and storing personal data, the value of personal data to businesses and individuals, and the potential risks, rewards, and ethics of selling personal data. Privacy economics also examines the economic impact of privacy laws and regulations, as well as the ways in which technology is changing the economics of privacy (Acquisti).

The Ethics of Data Trade

The trade, selling and purchasing of data is not an inherently bad or unethical practice. For some companies, purchasing data about their consumers allows them to adapt their marketing strategies, target their products to new buyers, or practice price discrimination. Some would argue that a company which understands their consumer is able to provide tailored customer service and a better overall experience. Take insurance companies for example – they collect and use your personal data in order to create a profile about you and predict the likelihood of you developing, for example, a debilitating illness (ABI). Insurance companies use data from a variety of sources – information provided by their customers, information readily available online, and information they buy from data brokers (ABI). Data brokers are companies that collect data from a wide range of sources and anonymize it. This information can be used to create more accessible and useful products, or to ensure accurate pricing. At times, this can be beneficial to a consumer, however, the line between harmless and harmful data trade is thin, and it is easy for this information to be used to benefit a company over a customer.

There are several potential drawbacks to the trade of personal data. For individuals, the main concern is that their personal information may be used without their knowledge or consent, or that it may be shared with organizations that they do not trust. It is well known that "market interactions involving personal data" rarely involve full and informed consent (Acquisti). When you sign the terms and agreements of a contract – whether or not you read it – you give permission for the collection and dissemination of your data in whatever legal ways that company sees fit to use it. However, this can lead to a loss of privacy and a lack of control over how one's personal data is used. Although you may agree to data sharing with 'third parties', who these third parties are is rarely divulged to the public. Additionally, there is the potential for personal data to be stolen or misused, which can lead to identity theft and other forms of fraud. This can have serious financial, legal, and personal consequences for victims of fraud.

Data Breaches and Identity Fraud

Virtually all data that is stored online can be hacked, meaning that an unauthorized person could gain access to that data. Hackers can obtain personal information through a data breach – an incident in which a large amount of data is accessed, copied, or used illegally by an unauthorized individual – but also by accessing information entered on a shared computer, an unsecured website or a public internet connection (Lockert).

Data breaches can have serious and sometimes irreversible consequences. Hackers can use the sensitive information they obtain to falsify documents, drain bank accounts and even impersonate people. These serious and illegal activities are generally grouped into the category of 'identity fraud' or 'identity theft'. Identity theft can be broken down into more specific categories, including: financial, medical, and synthetic identity theft (McAfee).

Financial identity theft pertains to all forms of fraud that involves accessing one's bank accounts and financials. If someone has gotten a hold of your debit or credit card information and PIN numbers, they could charge items to your cards, rack up debt on a stolen credit card, or drain your bank accounts. However, they could also use your personal information to open credit cards or take out loans in your name. While fraudulent bank transactions can sometimes be reversed, and new credit cards can be issues, financial identity theft can have serious impacts on your financial stability and credit score.

Medical identity theft occurs when a person obtains medical care, insurance, or prescription drugs under someone else's name. This can result in incorrect medical histories, or cause issues with insurance companies and premiums. Medical identity theft is one of the most common types of fraud in the

United States, impacting more than 48 million Americans in 2021 alone (McKeon).

Finally, synthetic identity fraud is one of the most complex types of identity fraud. According to forensic investigative accountant Jennifer Fiddian-Green, synthetic identity theft involves obtaining a person's social insurance number and assuming their identity (Mills). These sorts of thieves nurture these identities over significant periods of time by "establishing a history of income and gradually applying for more and more credit" (Mills). They often use a combination of real and fake information, and commonly use the information of children or people who are deceased, as that information is monitored less regularly and thus a crafted identity can be exploited for longer.

Should you unfortunately find yourself the victim of identity fraud of any type, you should contact your bank, the police, and your nearest anti-fraud Center. In Canada, the Canadian Anti-Fraud Call Center keeps open access records of all the reported and confirmed current fraud schemes, as well as offering support for reporting scams or fraud, and tips on how to protect oneself in the future. Further, should the scammer contact you again in order to extort you for more money in exchange for not sharing your personal information online, do not send the money. Fraudsters have been known to target a victim multiple times to continue their criminal activities. Don't fall for it!

The Biggest Cybersecurity Threats of 2021, 2022 and 2023

To end off this chapter, lets discuss the largest cybersecurity threats of 2022 and those predicted to be troubling in 2023. According to the commercial insurance company Embroker, the top three cybersecurity threats of 2022 included: social engineering, third party exposure, and configuration mistakes.

Social engineering, perhaps better known by the terms 'phishing', relies on human error rather than technological weakness (Embroker). In fact, according to the Verizon 2021 Data Breach Investigations Report, 85% of data breaches in 2021 were related to human error (Burbidge). Popular phishing scams include mass text messages that threaten legal action unless a fine is paid, or that encourage you to click on a link and update your security information for a website or subscription. These scams often look credible and target vulnerable people, such as the elderly, recent immigrants, or youth. In 2022, cryptocurrency scams skyrocketed, with many scammers hacking social media accounts on platforms like Instagram and Facebook (CNBCTV18.com). Once they gained access to a person's account, they would create fake posts claiming to have made thousands of dollars in quick-return crypto investments. Some would also message the individual's friends to market this get-rich quick scheme and manipulate the personal information divulged in those conversations to gain access to more social media accounts (CNBCTV18.com).

Third party exposure, or third party data breaches, occur when a hacker targets a third party company who had weaker security measures than their primary target, but who has "privileged access to the hacker's primary target" (Burbidge). In 2021, the third party contractor Socialarks was breached and the information of more than 214 million Facebook, Instagram and LinkedIn users were leaked (Burbidge).

Finally, according to Burbridge, almost every security software contains a configuration mistake – an exploitable error in how the software is installed or set up (Burbidge).

Industry leader Security Infowatch predicts that ransomware and cyber extortion will be the top threats of 2023 (Lasky). Some have hypothesized that Artificial Intelligence will also play a role in creating increasingly sophisticated phishing scams, especially with the impressive artificial technologies that have launched in the past year like OpenAI's Chat GPT (Lasky). Similarly, the idea of a super powerful quantum computer – which could become commercially available within the next decade – could threaten the encryptions which protect trade secrets, national security documents, and other sensitive intellectual data (Lasky).

Concluding Ideas

As we discussed in this chapter, personal security data is highly sensitive information that can be exploited in any number of creative and detrimental ways. The costs of data breaches are high, and can affect the financial and physical safety of millions of people. Thus, privacy laws are crucial tools necessary to protect individuals from online exploitation and identity theft, both in Canada and around the world. These laws help to regulate the ways organizations collect, store and trade data to ensure that personal information is handled with integrity.

The past year has seen an increase in cybercrime, phishing scams and the illegal dissemination of personal security information of millions of people. While technology continues to advance rapidly, it is important for individuals to stay informed about their rights regarding the collection and use of their personal data, and the ways in which they can avoid falling victim to scams and fraud. Further it is imperative that lawmakers worldwide remain vigilant in updating and enforcing privacy laws to keep pace with the changing landscape of the digital world.

References

ABI. (n.d.). Use of Data in Insurance. ABI. Retrieved December 31, 2022, from https://www.abi.org.uk/products-and-issues/topics-and-issues/data-and-the-digital-revolution/data-in-insurance/

Acquisti, A., Taylor, C., & Wagman, L. (2016). The Economics of Privacy. Journal of Economic Literature, 54(2), 442–492. https://doi.org/10.1257/jel.54.2.442

Burbidge, T. (2021, May 13). Cybercrime thrives during pandemic: Verizon 2021 Data Breach Investigations Report. Verizon. https://www.verizon.com/about/news/verizon-2021-data-breach-investigations-report

Clinen, E. (2022, July 1). Global Privacy Laws Explained. Privacy Policies. https://www.privacypolicies.com/blog/global-privacy-laws-explained/

CNBCTV18.com. (2022, October 8). Crypto scams rising on Instagram: A look at some common exploits and how to stay safe. Cnbctv18.Com. https://www.cnbctv18.com/cryptocurrency/crypto-scams-rising-on-instagram-some-of-the-common-exploits-how-to-stay-safe-14892741.htm

CSRC. (n.d.). PII - Glossary. Computer Security Resource Center. Retrieved December 13, 2022, from https://csrc.nist.gov/glossary/term/pii

Embroker. (2022, January 26). Top 10 Cybersecurity Threats in 2022 | Embroker. Embroker. https://www.embroker.com/blog/top-10-cybersecurity-threats-2022/

European Commission. (n.d.). What personal data is considered sensitive? European Commission. Retrieved December 31, 2022, from https://commission.europa.eu/law/law-topic/data-protection/reform/rules-business-and-organisations/legal-grounds-processing-data/sensitive-data/what-personal-data-considered-sensitive_en

Lasky, S. (2022, December 30). Ominous 2023 cybersecurity threats ensure an active landscape. Security Info Watch. https://www.securityinfowatch.com/cybersecurity/article/21291257/ominous-2023-cybersecurity-threats-ensure-an-active-landscape

Lockert, M. (2017, August 21). How do hackers use your information for identity theft? Credit Karma. https://www.creditkarma.com/id-theft/i/how-hackers-use-your-information

McAfee. (2022, July 16). 5 Common Types of Identity Theft. McAfee Blog. https://www.mcafee.com/blogs/privacy-identity-protection/5-common-types-of-identity-theft/

McKeon, J. (2022, December 20). This Year's Largest Healthcare Data Breaches. HealthITSecurity. https://healthitsecurity.com/features/this-years-largest-healthcare-data-breaches

Mills, S. (2022, April 19). Ottawa man faces mysterious income tax bill for employment he says he didn't have. CBC News. https://www.cbc.ca/news/canada/ottawa/mysterious-tax-bill-linked-to-synthetic-identity-fraud-1.6418589

Privacy Commissioner. (2014, May 15). Summary of privacy laws in Canada. Office of the Privacy Commissioner of Canada. https://www.priv.gc.ca/en/privacy-topics/privacy-laws-in-canada/02_05_d_15/#heading-0-0-2

UNCTAD. (n.d.). Data Protection and Privacy Legislation-Worldwide. United Nations Conference on Trade and Development. Retrieved December 15, 2022, from https://unctad.org/page/data-protection-and-privacy-legislation-worldwide

ANONYMITY IN RELATION TO PERSONAL SECURITY DATA

By David Henneberg

The differences between Anonymity, Privacy and Security

In the article "Privacy or Anonymity? Which is more important in the digital era?", it is stated that "technology is evolving quicker than most peoples' ability to understand it; therefore, it is increasingly critical to be safe online and to protect one's personal privacy." (Privacy or Anonymity, 2022) What does this all mean, and why would it be relevant? The purpose of this chapter is to educate the reader on the issues surrounding personal security data, the different types of security, the relevance of anonymity, the meaning of privacy, and ways that people can protect themselves better online.

First, what does anonymity mean? We will need to find a definition prior to our investigation into its relationship with personal data security. According to the Cambridge dictionary, the term anonymity can be used when "someone's name is not given or known." This means that although someone may not be identified, their actions can still be tracked. In short, anonymity is "when someone keeps their actions and activities separate from their identities." (Privacy or Anonymity, 2022)

There is a considerable difference between anonymity and privacy. Someone could have anonymity by creating a pseudonym and using it on a forum, for example. But anonymity would not guarantee privacy in any way, as privacy relates to the people that have access to information being shared. If the information is secure and can only be accessed by the parties that are authorised, then privacy would be considered secure. For the purposes of this argument, it is quite possible to have anonymity but not have any privacy. Therefore, privacy can be considered much more important than anonymity.

From the article "Privacy vs. Anonymity vs. Security: Why They Don't All Mean the Same Thing" Anina Ot says that "three of the most important concepts to understand are: privacy, anonymity, and security. But while most treat them as synonyms for having a safe digital presence, they don't mean the same thing. And depending on your online needs, you should prioritise one over the other." (Ot, 2021). Ot continues, "privacy is the ability to keep certain data and information about yourself exclusive to you and control who and what has access to it." (Ot, 2021)

At this point in time, we have a usable definition for anonymity and privacy, but what about security? "Security is a set of precautions and measures for protection against potential harm to your person and reputation, and files directly or indirectly from malicious parties." (Ot, 2021) These are the tangible steps being taken to mitigate risks from outside attacks on personal information and data. They can include things like antivirus software, encrypting files or using multi-factor authentication to log onto devices.

A quick summary of the differences between anonymity, privacy and security and when prioritising one over the other is useful:

Anonymity is the hiding of one's identity, but not necessarily keeping personal information and activities hidden. Privacy is the ability to manage what things people will see and read about an individual online, and security refers to the safeguards one might have (or should have) in place to stop malicious parties from gathering their personal data.

The type of protection an individual needs is situation dependent. In terms of privacy, it should be a "priority when using apps or services that have access to your personal information such as full name, email address, phone number, location, etc." (Ot, 2021) Anonymity should be a priority when a person does not want something tracked back to them. This can be helpful when people are "on online forums, expressing fringe political views, or exposing a public person or commercial entity's misconduct." (Ot, 2021) Security should be prioritised when a person has highly sensitive information, whether it be financial documents or private images. Things that could get leaked into the public sphere and ruin reputations and lives. These are generally the things to be concerned about when seeking security online.

The Current Views on Online Security

A lot of people look to online security companies to protect themselves from potential or real threats. Sadly, a lot of the time online security companies act like predators when selling products to people, advertising to protect security, privacy, or anonymity – and they are aware the consumer does not know the difference between the three (generally speaking). The amount of confusion over the matter is astonishing: "only 3 percent of Americans understand current online privacy regulations." (Vuleta, 2022) The simple fact of the matter is that these companies are taking advantage of how little the general population knows about personal data security. Anina Ot says "you need to understand what it means when software or an app says that they secure your data or pride themselves on offering complete privacy or anonymity. This allows you to pick the right option for your needs without falling prey to the halo effect of similar words.' (Ot, 2021)

Participating online has become not only common, but necessary in day-to-day life. From receiving and sending documents, online banking, to keeping up with your friends and family across the planet, everyone has a reason to be using the internet. Branka Vuleta mentions in her article "18 Chilling Privacy Statistics in 2022" that "everyone leaves a digital footprint whenever they use the internet. Our information is out there, from the most basic to sensitive data. With each passing day, the concept of privacy becomes thinner, while the risk of data breaches increases." (Vuleta, 2022). The concept of privacy becoming "thinner" is interesting to discuss. What exactly does Vuleta mean by that? Perhaps the population has become increasingly desensitised to online privacy and security. At this point it may seem pointless to fight against anonymity, privacy and security issues as corporations and governments battle to mine people's personal data. What is the point of trying to keep up with privacy, anonymity, and security when there are so many entities successfully gathering personal information? The old adage of "if you cannot beat them, join them" may be ringing true here. Has everyone given up on trying to keep their data safe? Has the population turned their wrists over to be forever handcuffed and enslaved?

"Most Americans feel they have little or no control over how government and private entities use their private information." (Sethumadhavan, 2021) According to a survey done by Pew Research Center of 500 adults, the general feeling of hopelessness is conveyed. This does not mean that people do not care about their privacy online, however. "Americans had strong views about privacy and wanted to have control over who can get information about them and what information is collected about them." (Sethumadhavan, 2021) According to "The Online Privacy Lie is Unraveling", an article written by Natasha Lomas, "a large majority of web users are not at all happy, but rather feel powerless to stop their data being harvested and used by marketers." (Lomas, 2015) The issue seems to be caught up in confusion.

Although there is a feeling of uncertainty around exactly how one protects themselves online, there seems to be a consensus that protection is vital. This leaves society in a grey area as it figures out how to deal with rapidly changing privacy laws and technological advancements. In the following sections of this chapter there will be a deeper dive into the current legislation in Canada and the U.S. and ways that individuals can protect themselves in terms of anonymity, privacy, and security.

Again, it is a difficult predicament the (entire) world finds itself in. According to Rainie et al. "59% of internet users do not believe it is possible to be completely anonymous online, while 37% of them believe it is possible" and "86% of internet users have taken steps online to remove or mask their digital footprints – ranging from clearing cookies to encrypting their email, from avoiding using their name to using virtual networks that mask their internet protocol (IP) address." (Rainie et al., 2013) The solution to our problems must involve "meaningful consent" which would "facilitate user understanding while preventing information overload..." (Sethumadhavan, 2021)

Reasons To Take Online Data Privacy Seriously

There are many sobering facts about online privacy. According to "10 Online Privacy Facts That May Surprise You" by Susan Alexandra, "21% of online users are the victim of account hacking" and "11% of online users have been the victim of data theft." (Alexandra, 2019) This information that has been stolen includes social media accounts, credit cards and social security numbers. The unfortunate part is that many cases could have been prevented with a little proactive work in properly protecting the three pillars of anonymity, privacy, and security.

One often overlooked area of our online security is the amount of trust we put in other parties to be careful with our information. One does not have to look very far back in time to see the incredible amount of data breaches occurring regularly with user data. In 2021 alone there were multiple breaches that impacted over 500 million user records per breach. (Komnenic, 2022) That is a significant percentage of the world's population having its data breached regularly! No wonder people can feel so hopeless in terms of online security. It has become a regular occurrence on a scale that is impossibly large to comprehend. According to Komnenic in regard to the biggest data breach of 2020, "hackers scraped Facebook due to a security gap that the company had patched back in 2019. As a result, 533,000,000 user records from 106 countries were posted on a hacking forum. The leaked information included user locations, full names, biographical information, phone numbers, and email addresses." (Komnenic, 2022)

It is obvious at this point that we have a problem so large in scope it could be impossible to address. The next chapter will start to outline the current laws and legislation in relation to these issues, and try to get to the bottom of solutions for legislation as well as protective solutions for individuals. The hope is that it becomes easier for individuals to protect themselves and for companies to become more transparent.

Current Legislation In Regard To Personal Data Security

According to the Office of the Privacy Commissioner of Canada's website, one should always ask the following questions (Protecting Your Privacy Online, 2018):

- Who is collecting the information?

- Is it necessary for the transaction?

- What will be done with it?

- What are the consequences for me?

The answers to these questions can be found in a myriad of places. The email provider's privacy policy, terms of use agreement or other privacy communications provided by the company. If one cannot get answers to these questions, one should consider taking their business elsewhere. There are so many ways for a person to be scammed online for malicious purposes that it is not worth the risk if there is any uncertainty at all. In 2021, 379 million dollars of Canadian's money was scammed from fraudsters - the vast majority of the scams targeted online (DaSilva, 2021).

The case of anonymity online has been a turbulent one at times, especially for police trying to investigate online crimes. If a person is involved in illegal acts under an anonymous name it can prove to be difficult for investigators to gather information. "The Supreme Court of Canada said anonymity is vital to personal privacy in the digital era. It told police they need a judge's permission before asking Internet providers for basic information that would identify their customers - such as a suspected child pornographer at the heart of a ... investigation." (Fine, 2014) This case was perhaps a landmark in terms of online anonymity. The police are unable to gather personal information on an anonymous individual without consent from a judge (a warrant). This poses a problem for the police while making sure the basic right to anonymity is protected by consumers. Personal anonymity is deemed to be more important than a police officer's ability to freely collect personal information.

Think about all the places personal information is now stored online. Here is a quick and no-so-thorough list:
- Online stores (Amazon, Etsy, etc.)
- Banks
- Communications companies (Shaw, Telus, etc.)
- Food delivery services
- Insurance and health providers

The list could go on ad-infinitum. There are a plethora of places that are storing private and personal information online. This is why there has been a need to develop cybersecurity laws. "Cybersecurity laws - including data protection and privacy legislation - are laws that aim to safeguard information technology and computer systems from privacy breaches and unauthorised activity as well as to compel corporations and organisations to protect their online infrastructure from cyber attacks." (Lukings and Habibi, 2020) These laws are in place simply because consumers' information is important, and individual companies must be held responsible for the safe-keeping of personal data.

To understand a little bit more about legislation and online privacy, it is important to take a look at how Canadian law is formed. "The two main sources of Canadian law are the legislation - including Acts and statutes - and the Common Law - which refers to previous judicial decisions in cases with similar facts and matters." (Lukings and Habibi, 2020) This means that there are both written laws that are passed through legislation as well as laws that come into effect based on previous legal proceedings. The latter is quite important because the online world is moving at an incredible pace, and the ability for the law to be updated on a case-by-case basis is most important and practical... otherwise the law would be constantly antiquated as laws that were being held up in parliament were being processed. This ensures that only the latest and most pertinent information is shaping the laws in Canadian society. The common law applies to the aforementioned case of the judge's ruling in the child pornography case. The common law is constantly in flux and under revision and so it is increasingly important for individuals to do their research on what the current laws are, and which cases might be most applicable to them.

Maintaining Anonymity Online

Although many parties are interested in gathering personal information and individual identities, it is possible to protect oneself from an intrusive collector. This does not mean it is simple and easy, however. "The truth is, unless you make a concerted effort, you have no privacy or anonymity online. For those who want it, online anonymity is possible; however, it's not the most straightforward process..." (Vigderman and Turner, 2022) In the article "How To Remain Anonymous on the Internet" by Aliza Vigderman and Gabe Turner a 22 step process is outlined. This process, however tedious, ensures that an individual remains anonymous. It is important to remember that in this day and age a concerted effort is needed to fully protect oneself. If these steps are not taken then information is guaranteed to permeate into data miners' hands.

Here is the 22-step process (paraphrased), as outlined by Vigderman and Turner:
• Use an encrypted messaging app. iMessage is encrypted and so is WhatsApp... but there are also other apps that guarantee the same level of security (like Signal, Viber, etc.).

• Use an encrypted browser. Tor is recommended. Chrome by Google is "notorious" for collecting, using and selling users' data.

• Use a VPN. Or Virtual Private Network. This hides all web traffic information from all parties involved. From the web-sites being visited to the internet service provider that hosts the internet connection.

• Use secure email services. Gmail (Google) keeps all pri-vate emails and information on their own encrypted servers, which they have access to. Vigderman and Turner recom-mend using ProtonMail, which is based out of Switzerland. This would be a neutral entity that would not give over access of personal emails to government officials.

• Use a temporary email. This is handy for giving email ad-dresses for newsletters or annoying subscriptions. Temp Mail is a service that provides temporary email addresses.

• Use encrypted storage. Stopping using Google services is becoming a common theme. It is recommended to use a storage service that does not keep or share data, like Sync or Tresorit.

• Don't post Personal Identifiable Information. Like a social security number.

The rest of the steps will be written out, but only a few of them will be covered with any detail.
• Check App Permissions.

• Read Privacy Policies.

• Use ad Blockers

• Don't use voice assistants

• Stay off Social Media. Easier said than done, but sound advice. Social media is a haven for the sale of private infor-mation.

• Use a proxy

• Check for HTTPS

• Disable cookies

- Don't use Google. It has been mentioned prior. Google is notorious for gathering information for profit.

- Use a password manager.

- Use a secure operating system

- Use anonymous cryptocurrency. Bitcoin, for example, is traceable to the user. There are cryptocurrencies that are untraceable.

- Disable JavaScript

- Avoid Spam

- Use a file shredder. Information that is thrown in the "trash can" of a computer is still recoverable. A file shredder will jumble up the data behind the file so that it is incomprehensible for software to put back together.

Based on the 22-step process it takes to maintain complete anonymity online, one could say it is a difficult task. The current gold rush of the 21st century is the data mining of human activity online. Companies want to figure out how to maintain the attention of the general population for as long as possible since every second of engagement - every click, like, follow, subscription - is worth real dollars. There is a real battle over personal information taking place between consumers and companies whether the consumer is aware or not. And the motivation behind this corporate behaviour is quite simple and has been well-known for a very long time. Here is an excerpt from the Harvard Business Review printed in 1997. "Companies have good reason(s) to collect information about customers. It enables them to target their most valuable prospects more effectively, tailor their offerings to individual needs, improve customer satisfaction and retention, and identify opportunities for new products or services." (Hagel III and Rayport, 1997)

Summary

Although the task at hand of keeping anonymity online and personal security data private seems daunting, it should be clear that if no steps are taken to mitigate the risks, then private information is being distributed. And this private information that is being distributed is highly valuable to companies - and so the real question is this: why are consumers giving away their data freely, without any kind of return? It is hoped that this chapter helps the reader reflect on their own online anonymity, privacy and security, and opens the door for them to start taking steps in the direction of protecting themselves. The next section will dive even deeper into the best practices to protect oneself online.

References

Alexandra, S. (2019, July 10). 10 online privacy facts that May surprise you. My TechDecisions. Retrieved December 22, 2022, from https://mytechdecisions.com/network-security/10-online-privacy-facts/

DaSilva, T. (2021, December 31). Costly Scams Rob Canadians of Hundreds of Millions of Dollars in 2021.

Fine, S. (2014, June 13). Canadians have right to online anonymity, Supreme Court rules. The Globe and Mail. Retrieved December 22, 2022, from https://www.theglobeandmail.com/news/national/supreme-court-privacy/article19155295/

Hagel, J., & Rayport, J. F. (1997, January). The Coming Battle for Consumer Information. Harvard Business Review.

Lomas, N. (2015, June 6). The Online Privacy Lie is unraveling.

TechCrunch. Retrieved December 22, 2022, from https://techcrunch.com/2015/06/06/the-online-privacy-lie-is-unraveling/

Lukings, M., & Habibi Lashkari, A. (2021). Legal foundations. Understanding Cybersecurity Law and Digital Privacy, 1–35. https://doi.org/10.1007/978-3-030-88704-9_1

Masha Komnenic CIPP/E, C. I. P. M. (2022, November 17). 98 biggest data breaches, hacks, and exposures [2022 update]. Termly. Retrieved December 22, 2022, from https://termly.io/resources/articles/biggest-data-breaches/

Office of the Privacy Commissioner of Canada. (2018, August 23). Protecting your privacy online. Office of the Privacy Commissioner of Canada. Retrieved December 22, 2022, from https://www.priv.gc.ca/en/privacy-topics/technology/online-privacy-tracking-cookies/online-privacy/protecting-your-privacy-online/

Ot, A. (2021, March 20). Privacy vs. anonymity vs. security: Why they don't all mean the same thing. MUO. Retrieved December 22, 2022, from https://www.makeuseof.com/privacy-anonymity-security-mean/

Perekalin, A., Grustniy, L., Kaminsky, S., Starikova, A., & Team, K. (n.d.). How to improve privacy online in 10 easy steps. Daily English Global blogkasperskycom. Retrieved December 22, 2022, from https://www.kaspersky.com/blog/privacy-ten-tips-2018/23022/

Rainie, L. (2020, August 17). Anonymity, privacy, and security online. Pew Research Center: Internet, Science & Tech. Retrieved December 22, 2022, from https://www.pewresearch.org/internet/2013/09/05/anonymity-privacy-and-security-online/

Sethumadhavan, A. (2021, October 8). Do people even care about data privacy in the Digital age? Big Think. Retrieved December 22, 2022, from https://bigthink.com/the-present/data-privacy-statistics/

Vigderman, A. (2022, October 14). How to remain anonymous on the internet. Security.org. Retrieved December 22, 2022, from https://www.security.org/vpn/anonymity/

Vuleta, B. (2022, January 17). 18 chilling privacy statistics in 2022. Find Best Law Jobs in the US in 2022. Retrieved December 22, 2022, from https://legaljobs.io/blog/privacy-statistics/

BEST PRACTICES FOR AVERAGE CONSUMERS

By Michael Phan

In this digital age where one's entire life is on their phone or computer, it has become more and more important to protect one's data. For instance, it has been reported that up to ninety percent of Canadians have been using online banking to carry out the majority of their banking transactions (Canadian Banking Association 2019). However, it was also reported that at least forty two percent of Canadians have experienced at least one of many cybersecurity incidents – including, but not limited to, phishing, fraudulent or compromised accounts, and viruses (Government of Canada 2021).

With the abundance of sensitive information that consumers have floating around the limitless internet, this means that it is very likely that there will be an attempt by a third party entity to access it. Using this personal data, one would then be able to cause, sometimes irreparable, damage. If a scammer were able to access someone's bank account through their leaked banking credentials, they would be able to transfer money out and into their own account. This can also lead to identity theft, where the scammer is even able to open up new accounts and apply for credit cards all under the name of the victim (Hinde 2005). Indeed, identity theft is a real issue – with the Canadian Anti-Fraud Centre reporting an estimated one in five Canadians that could be victims of identity theft, and Equifax reporting that more than half of Canadians have been victims of any variety of financial fraud (Equifax 2016).

This is why it is incredibly important for the average consumer to protect themselves from identity theft by being vigilant about their personal information. There are many facets in which the average consumer is able to protect themselves from identity theft. Many of which do not involve much extra effort from the consumer's end. One way to mitigate the risk of data breaches is to ensure that the quality (and quantity) of passwords are sufficient. To make a good password, one must ensure that their passcode is at least eight characters long while containing a varied assortment of upper case and lower case letters, numbers, and special characters such as the semi colon, an exclamation mark, or an apostrophe, just to name a few. In their passwords, consumers should also avoid using complete words or phrases, as well as sequences of numbers (i.e., 1, 2, 3, 4, 5, 6, 7, 8, etc). As it turns out, the world's most commonly used password was "password," with "123456" being the second most commonly used password (Piñon 2022). While often tedious, it is also a good idea for people to consistently change or modify their passwords regularly, while also having multiple passwords for their different accounts. In order to keep track of the multitudes of passwords, or even get help generating unique and effective passwords, people will often use password managers such as Google Password Manager.

Another way for the average consumer to protect their data is by using two step authentication (otherwise known as two factor authentication) for their accounts containing sensitive data. For this method, as the name suggests, there are two particular steps that are necessary before being able to sign into any given account. After the password is inputted, which is the first step, the user is then prompted to fill in a box asking for a unique code. This code can either be retrieved after being sent to the user's email address, phone number, or through an authentication app. The effectiveness of this method lies in the second step, since it is not very likely at all for a hacker to have access to either the email address, phone number, or the authentication app as well as the original password.

By their very nature, being public and unencrypted, public Wi-Fi networks are often vulnerable to cyber attacks on the average consumer by hackers. This implies that any data sent or received across the network can be intercepted by anybody else on the network. Hackers can use tools to monitor network traffic and get access to sensitive information such as passwords, credit card numbers, and other personal information. Furthermore, public Wi-Fi networks are frequently unprotected, which means that they do not require a password to access, leaving them even more open to assault. Thus, it is in the average consumer's best interest to avoid using public Wi-Fi especially when handling sensitive or financial data.

Virtual Private Networks (VPNs) are private networks that connect different sites or users over a public network, frequently the internet. It essentially allows users to send and receive data over shared or public networks almost as if their computer systems were physically directly tied to a private network. VPNs can be used to avoid territorial limitations on internet content and enable a secure connection to a company's internal network. What makes it useful? A Virtual private network is important because it allows two or more devices to communicate securely over the internet. This essentially means that data that is transmitted across the connection is encrypted, making it considerably more difficult for hackers or other criminal elements to intercept and look at the information. A Virtual private network may also be used to circumvent geographical limitations, allowing users to access content that may not be readily accessible in their present location. Finally, a Virtual private network may be used to help hide a user's IP address, thereby making it much more difficult for websites or services to monitor the user's online behavior. However, virtual private networks can still be insecure. They may indeed be insecure if it is not properly configured and monitored. It is essential that you choose a reliable VPN provider with robust encryption and other security features. Furthermore, users should always use the most recent version of the VPN software and ensure that their device is safe with the most recent anti-virus and anti-malware software.

On the topic of anti-virus and anti-malware software, it is important to maintain these two facets since they enable the average consumer to protect their data. Anti-virus and anti-malware software's primary function is to safeguard personal computers and networks from harmful cyber attacks (NCSC 2019). Malware refers to any variety of exploitational software, which would include viruses, worms, Trojans, and spyware. Not only are these malicious applications capable of causing identity theft, but they can also lead to a much wider range of issues, including data loss and system failures. By searching for and deleting harmful applications, anti-virus and anti-malware software helps to guard against these dangers. Anti-virus and anti-malware software detects harmful applications by scanning a computer or network (NCSC 2019). This is accomplished by comparing files and programmes on the computer or network to a database of dangerous applications that are already identified as malicious. If a match is detected, the malicious application will be quarantined or deleted by the software. It will also notify the user of the harmful program's presence and give information on how to delete it. Anti-virus and anti-malware software are critical for safeguarding PCs and networks from harmful intrusions (NCSC 2019). It is critical to investigate and evaluate the many services available in order to discover the biggest and best fit for your requirements. By following these procedures, you may assist to protect the safety and security of your computer and network.

Ad-blockers are a variety of downloadable software that restrict advertising from being displayed on websites and other online platforms. They are growing more popular as even more people are becoming conscious of the potential harm that advertisements could very well cause. Ad-blockers can protect users against harmful advertising that contain dangerous code or redirect to hazardous websites. They may also be employed to prevent unwanted or obnoxious advertisements, such as pop-up adverts or auto-play ads. Ad-blockers may also be used to prevent advertisements from certain businesses or websites, allowing consumers to tailor their online experience. Ad-blocking software is available for installation on personal computers, tablets, mobile phones, and web browsers. They are generally freely available to download, but many are incorporated into web browsers

Clicking on dodgy websites or downloading unauthorised files may very well put the average consumer's computer and personal data in harm's way. Cybercriminals are continuously seeking for new methods to abuse naïve individuals and steal their personal information. You may expose your computer to malicious software, such as viruses, spyware, or ransomware, by clicking on a potentially malicious link or downloading an unfamiliar file. Your personal information, including passwords, financial information, and credit card numbers, can be obtained by this dangerous programme. Clicking on dubious links or downloading unfamiliar files can lead to phishing attacks in addition to the danger of harmful malware. Cybercriminals seek to acquire access to your personal information by sending you emails or text messages that look to be from a genuine source. These communications may include links or files that, when clicked or downloaded, could perhaps download malicious software or move you to something like a dangerous website. In light of this, it is essential to refrain from clicking on strange links or downloading unexpected files. If you encounter an email or text message that looks to be from a genuine source, double-check the sender before clicking any links or downloading any attachments. Also, keep your computer and software up to date with the most recent security updates and antivirus software. You can help protect your computer and personal data against malicious malware and other security threats by following these steps.

Phishing and social engineering are cyber attack strategies that utilize misinformation to deceive individuals into disclosing their personal information or doing certain activities. The simplest example of phishing generally involves emails that appear to be from a genuine source, such as a financial institution or an online merchant, in order to fool the receiver into opening a link that is suspicious or disclosing sensitive information. The phrase "social engineering" refers to any sort of attack that uses psychological manipulation to mislead victims. Impersonating a trusted source, establishing a feeling of urgency, and leveraging human curiosity are all common social engineering strategies (Federal Trade Commission 2019).

Knowing the different kinds of phishing scams and how to spot them is crucial if you want to avoid falling for any one of the variety and multitude, as well as diversity, of phishing scams (Federal Trade Commission 2019). As mentioned above, email phishing is one of the most popular forms of phishing scams. This scam usually involves sending an email that pretends to be from a genuine source, such as a bank or other financial organization, and requests personal information or money. These emails frequently contain links to dangerous websites or files that can infect your machine with harmful software. To prevent being a victim of an email phishing scam, be suspicious of any emails that request personal information or money. Do not open any attachments or click on any links in emails you receive from unknown senders (Federal Trade Commission 2019). SMS phishing is another kind of phishing fraud that includes sending text messages that look to be from a reputable source. These messages frequently contain links to fraudulent websites or attachments that might download malware on your phone or personal computer. Any text messages that request personal information or money should be avoided in order to prevent falling for an SMS phishing scam. Avoid clicking on any links or opening any attachments if you receive a text message from an unidentified sender. You may protect yourself from becoming a victim of a phishing scam by being aware of the many types of phishing scams and how to spot them. Always be wary of emails, text messages, social media communications, or phone calls from unfamiliar people, and never give out personal information or money.

Being vigilant about the personal information that you publish on the internet is also a way for the average consumer to protect their data. Without a doubt, it is increasingly crucial to safeguard your personal information from identity theft or fraud. You may lower the possibility of somebody of mischievous and suspicious nature from having access to your personal information, such as your Social Security number, credit card numbers, or bank account information, by being cautious about what you disclose online. Furthermore, being cautious of what you share online is always a good idea because of the fact that it can have a long term influence on your reputation. As an example, if one were to publish a certain particular post that could be deemed as perhaps rude or improper, future employers, family, and friends may come across it. It is thus critical to remember that once something is uploaded online, it is difficult to erase and can be spread with a large audience. As a result, it is critical to think twice before sharing anything online and to consider the potential ramifications of your actions. It's also important to acknowledge how businesses and organisations take advantage of your data. Many businesses and organisations acquire personal information from users in order to tailor adverts to them or track their online activities. You may limit the chance of your data being used in ways you did not intend by being cautious about what you disclose online.

Keeping your computer up to date with the newest versions of any particular or given software is one of the most important steps you can undertake to make sure that your personal data is safe and secure. You can secure your data against the latest security risks by frequently upgrading your software.

Software updates provide key security updates that are designed to protect your system from malicious attacks. These software updates can greatly assist in the protection of your data from hackers, malware, and other dangerous applications. Your system is vulnerable to attack without such upgrades, and your data may be compromised. To secure your personal data, it is critical to maintain your software up to date.

Additionally, significant bug fixes and performance improvements are provided through software upgrades. You can verify that your system is working properly and that your data is secure from any problems by upgrading your software. Outdated software can lead to system dysfunction and data loss or even damage. Keeping your software up to date might assist to prevent these problems and protect the security of your data.

Access to new features and functionality is also provided through software upgrades. By upgrading your programme, you can gain access to new features and tools that can enhance your experience. New features can help your system run more efficiently and secure your data. What is also very substantially crucial to note is that software upgrades are not always free. Some software upgrades are either provided on a subscription basis or require a one time cost. It is important to look into the cost of software upgrades before you purchase them. This will assist to guarantee that you are getting the most bang for your buck and that your data is safe. Finally, keep in mind that software upgrades might be time-consuming. It is critical to set aside time on a regular basis to update your software. This ensures that your system is constantly up to date and that your data is protected.

Choosing a trustworthy web browser can also help to secure the data of the average consumer. Many browsers have extra security capabilities, such as private browsing, that can aid in the protection of a user's personal information. Furthermore, certain browsers provide enhanced security against fraudulent websites, phishing efforts, and other security risks. Users may help protect the safety and security of their data by taking the time to investigate and pick a secure browser. Users should update their browsers on a regular basis to take advantage of the most recent security updates and fixes. Outdated browsers may have vulnerabilities that hackers may exploit, therefore it is critical to maintain them up to date. It is also advised to use a browser with a proven track record of security and privacy, as well as a trustworthy corporation backing it. Finally, when browsing the internet, individuals may further secure their data by utilising a virtual private network (VPN), which can help encrypt their data and mask their location. Users may take an active role in preserving their data and maintaining their online privacy by following these measures.

It is also critical in today's digital era to be vigilant about the websites that you visit and the personal data that you provide. With the development of the internet, accessing information and connecting with people has become simpler than ever. However, this implies that hostile entities have more opportunity to acquire your personal information and use it for their own advantage (Sectigo 2020). Although many websites could have a trustworthy appearance, they might really be created with the intent to steal your personal data. Before entering any personal information, such as your name, address, or credit card information, it is critical to conduct research on any website. Furthermore, it is critical to be wary of phishing scams, which are efforts to get your personal information by impersonating a real firm or organisation (Sectigo 2020). It is also critical to understand the privacy rules of the websites you frequent. Many websites will gather and utilise your personal information for marketing reasons. To understand how your information will be used, read the privacy policies of every website you visit (Sectigo 2020). Furthermore, it is critical to be aware of the security procedures that websites employ to secure your information. Many websites will utilise encryption to secure your data, but some will not.

As it stands, the greatest internet security precautions include using strong and complex passwords, avoiding public Wi-Fi networks, utilising two factor authentication, and being extremely cautious and wary of phishing schemes. It is also important to keep your software and operating systems up to date, to use a secure online browser, and to be cautious about the websites you visit and the information you give. You can assist maintain the security of your personal data online by following these best practices.

References

Canadian Banking Association. 2019. "Focus: How Canadians Bank." Cba.ca. 2019. https://cba.ca/technology-and-banking.

Equifax. 2016. "Financial Fraud Survey." The Research intelligence Group. https://www.dropbox.com/s/c8jets3n-suemw0o/Equifax%20Report_Feb%2029%202016_Final.pdf?dl=0.

Federal Trade Commission. 2019. "How to Recognize and Avoid Phishing Scams." Consumer Information. May 3, 2019. https://consumer.ftc.gov/articles/how-recognize-and-avoid-phishing-scams.

Government of Canada, Statistics Canada. 2021. "The Daily — Canadian Internet Use Survey, 2020." Www150.Statcan. gc.ca. June 22, 2021. https://www150.statcan.gc.ca/n1/daily-quotidien/210622/dq210622b-eng.htm.

Hinde, Stephen. 2005. "Identity Theft: Theft, Loss and Giveaways." Computer Fraud & Security 2005 (5): 18–20. https://doi.org/10.1016/s1361-3723(05)70215-3.

NCSC. 2019. "What Is an Antivirus Product? Do I Need One?" Www.ncsc.gov.uk. January 21, 2019. https://www.ncsc.gov.uk/guidance/what-is-an-antivirus-product#:~:text=An%20 antivirus%20product%20is%20a.

Piñon, Natasha. 2022. "Hackers Guessed the World's Most Common Password in under 1 Second—Make Sure Yours Isn't on the List." CNBC. November 23, 2022. https://www.cnbc.com/2022/11/23/most-common-passwords-of-2022-make-sure-yours-isnt-on-the-list.html.

Sectigo. 2020. "Sectigo." Sectigo.com. November 5, 2020. https://sectigo.com/resource-library/what-happens-when-i-visit-a-malicious-website.

BREACH EXAMPLES

By Alicia Au

Introduction

In this chapter, we will explore examples of breaches of personal security data. In Canada, organizations, large and small, that are " subject to the Personal Information Protection and Electronic Documents Act (PIPEDA) are required to report to the Privacy Commissioner of Canada breaches of security safeguards involving personal information that pose a real risk of significant harm to individuals, notify affected individuals about those breaches, and keep records of all breaches" (Office of the Privacy Commissioner of Canada, 2018). A report by Arkose Labs, revealed that the frequency of security breaches has increased by 20% in comparison to 2019 (Arkose Labs, 2020). This means that every 11 seconds, there is an attack in any part of the world. A couple of these examples will be explored, with the largest ones prioritized. Key events that led up to these data breaches and the consequences will be examined.

Facebook

Facebook was rocked by controversy over Cambridge Analytica, a political consulting firm that had obtained private data from as many as 87 million Facebook users for what appeared to help Donald Trump win the presidency (Confessore, 2018).

March 2014

According to The Times, the largest known Facebook data leak occurred in 2014 when Cambridge Analytica's contractors and employees acquired the private Facebook data of tens of millions of users in order to sell psychological profiles of American voters to political campaigns (Rosenberg et al., 2018a).

An article by The New York Times, first described how Cambridge, which may have been a violation of American election law, received warnings from its attorney, Laurence Levy, over the use of Europeans and Canadian people on campaign staff (Rosenberg et al., 2018b). The Times discovered that portions of unprocessed data continued to reside outside of Facebook's control.

The Times also revealed in a related article that executives from the Kremlin-affiliated oil company Lukoil spoke with representatives of Cambridge Analytica and its British subsidiary, the SCL Group, while Cambridge developed its Facebook-derived profiles (Hakim & Rosenberg, 2018). According to two former corporate officials, Lukoil was interested in the methods used to target American voters using data. The oil firm never because a customer, according to SCL and Lukoil, who further disputed that the discussions were political in nature.

These publications immediately sparked a response in Washington, where Mark Zuckerberg, Facebook's CEO, appeared before Congress (Rosenberg & Frenkel, 2018). Democrats who are investigating Russian meddling in the 2016 election and who are already interested in Cambridge's role in supplying analytics to the Trump campaign declared they would investigate into the leak. They were repeated by British legislators looking into Cambridge Analytica's role in spreading false information and the nation's vote to quit the European Union.

According to The Times, Cambridge's chief executive, Alexander Nix, was placed on administrative leave after a British television network aired an undercover film in which he claimed the business had used seduction and bribery to entrap politicians and sway international elections(Rosenberg, 2018a). The Federal Trade Commission in Washington initiated an investigation to see whether Facebook had transgressed its initial promise to protect user data.

The Times reported on an increasing number of Facebook users deleting their accounts, including singer Cher (Hsu, 2018). The publication also broke the news of the departure of Facebook's top security official, who had argued with other executives about how to handle complaints about the social media site's role in spreading misinformation. On Twitter, the #DeleteFacebook started to trend.

The connection between Cambridge Analytica and John Bolton, the republican hawk appointed national security adviser by President Trump, was investigated as Facebook sputtered (Rosenberg, 2018b). It was initially reported that Cambridge delivered early copies of its Facebook-derived profiles to Mr. Bolton's "super PAC" in 2014, marking the technology's first significant application in an American election.

Another article by The Times detailed how a worker at Palantir Technologies, an intelligence contractor established by Trump supporter and tech entrepreneur Peter Thiel, assisted Cambridge Analytica in gathering Facebook data (Confessore & Rosenberg, 2018). According to the story, Cambridge briefly discussed forming a formal alliance to collaborate on political campaigns. Even though the transaction failed, a Palantir staff member kept in touch with Cambridge to figure out how to gather information for psychographic profiles. Officials from Palantir claimed that the individual acted only for personal reasons.

April

Initially, The Times said that Cambridge had collected information from more than 5- million Facebook users. However, Facebook's chief technical officer, Nike Schroepfer, provided a revised estimate for the number of people who were impacted: as many as 87 million, with the majority of them in the United States, at the bottom of a company release on new privacy improvements (Kang & Frenkel, 2018).

Facebook users whose data was harvested stayed conspicuously silent during the crisis. The Times managed to track down several, and their responses to the way that tech firms use personal information ranged from rage to resignation (Rosenberg & Dance, 2018).

New information regarding the app used to gather data for Cambridge Analytica was also disclosed by The Times (Rosenberg & Dance, 2018). As many had believed, it was not a straightforward Facebook quiz. Instead, it was an addendum to a lengthy psychology survey that was hosted by the internet survey management business Qualtrics. Giving access to their Facebook profiles was the first requirement for individuals to complete the questionnaire. After they done so, an app collected their data as well as those of their friends.

In his first appearance before Congress, Mr. Zuckerberg testified before Senate and House committees (Roose & Kang, 2018). First up was the Senate, where he was grilled about the company's data management practices and said that

Facebook was looking at "tens of thousands of apps" to find out what data they were harvesting.

He had to deal with a tougher crowd in the House the next day (Kang & Roose, 2018). There, it was widely agreed that social media technology had far overtaken Washington, and its potential for abuse, and that Congress may have to step in to bridge the gap. Even Mark Zuckerberg appeared to hint that he would be amenable to some regulation, but neither he nor the politicians appeared to be certain of the precise details of how to manage the new breed of businesses.

Today

According to The New York Times, copies of the data collected by Cambridge Analytica can still be available online (Cadwalladr & Graham-Harrison, 2018). Members of the reporting team had access to some of the raw data. Thisisyourdigitallife, an app created by academic Aleksandr Kogan apart from his work at Cambridge University, was used to obtain the data. Hundreds of thousands of people were paid to take a personality test through his company Global Science Research (GSR), in partnership with Cambridge Analytica, and agreed to have their data gathered for academic purpose (Cadwalladr & Graham-Harrison, 2018).

Concerns regarding Facebook's participation in selecting voters for the US presidential election have become even more pressing in light of the revelation of the unprecedented data collecting and the purposes for which it was used (Cadwalladr & Graham-Harrison, 2018). It comes just after Robert Mueller's special counsel indicted 13 Russians, charging them with using the platform to engage in "information warfare" against the US (Cadwalladr & Graham-Harrison, 2018).

More than 2 years after the data breach was initially discovered, Facebook stated that it has suspended Cambridge Analytica and Kogan from using its platform while it investigated any data misuse (Grewal, 2018). Separately, Facebook's outside attorneys informed that its claims were "false and defamatory" and reserved Facebook's legal stance (Grewal, 2018).

The majority of American states, including California, where Facebook is headquartered, have laws requiring notification in some instances of data breaches (Cadwalladr & Graham-Harrison, 2018).

Facebook disputes the claim that GSR and Cambridge Analytica's collection of tens of millions of profiles constituted a data breach (Cadwalladr & Graham-Harrison, 2018). Kogan "obtained access to this information in a legal manner and through the appropriate procedures," the company claimed in a statement, but "did not afterwards adhere by our standards" since he disclosed the data to outside parties (Cadwalladr & Graham-Harrison, 2018).

After the Cambridge Analytica scandal emerged, Zuckerberg did make a number of explicit promises (Wong, 2019). When the UK's Information Commissioner's Office (ICO) launched its own investigation, Facebook withdrew from its plans to conduct a forensic audit of Cambridge Analytica and other companies implicated in the data misuse, as it had announced on March 19, 2018. On March 13, a Facebook spokesperson stated that the business was still awaiting the ICO's authority to conduct any such audit (Wong, 2019). In a statement made on March 21, 2018, Facebook CEO Mark Zuckerberg pledged to look into "any applications that had access to huge quantities of information" through the network prior to 2014, examine any questionable behaviour in an app, and remove any developers who mishandled personally identifiable information (Wong, 2019). Up until August 22, 2018, when the corporation said in a blog post that it had reviewed thousands of third-party applications and suspended "more than 400," Facebook published regular updates on its inquiry (Archibong, 2018). Seven months later, a representative offered the same figures of thousands under investigation, more than 400 banned while stating that the inquiry was still ongoing. On May 1, Facebook announced the development of a "clear history" feature that would enable users to order Facebook to remove all the data it collects about them while they surf the internet (Egan, 2018). Facebook stated at the time that the tool would "take a few months to create." It has been a lot more than a few months, as BuzzFeed News noted in February (Mac, 2019). A Facebook spokesperson said that it was taking time to perfect the tool but did not give a timeframe for when it may really be made accessible(Wong, 2019).

The tilt to "privacy," revealed, is the second key promise (Wong, 2019). Contrary to what Zuckerberg insinuated, the real specifics of this strategy are far more routine and entail considerably less true privacy. The CEO intends to combine all three of his company's messaging services—WhatsApp, Instagram, and Messenger—into a single one that will support end-to-end encryption. The vast majority of privacy experts agree that this approach is mostly about maintaining market dominance and has nothing to do with preserving privacy. When you consider the upcoming regulatory pressures around interoperability and data-portability, the switch to encrypted messaging or "delete history" makes sense, according to Soltani (Wong, 2019). "They are incredibly adept at strategically using privacy as a justification for an anticompetitive strategy," he added. The concept of pursuing anti-trust action against Facebook, which is growing in popularity and has quickly moved from the periphery of the thinktank world to the heart of the agenda of a significant 2020 Democratic presidential contender, is the most overt of these looming pressures (Smith, 2019).

Amazon

December 2014

Credit card numbers and expiration dates, and 13,000 user-names and password combinations for websites such as Amazon, Walmart, PlayStation Network and others were exposed in December 2014 by hackers affiliated with the hacktivist group Anonymous (Kumar, 2014). Though they did declare their motivation in a tweet: "A total of approximately 13k accounts. We did for the Lulz," it is unclear from where or how they received this information (Kumar, 2014).

2016

Wired revealed in November 2021 that it was a regular practice for Amazon staff to monitor customer's purchase history back in 2016 (Evans, 2021). One manager said, "Everybody, everybody did it" (Evans, 2021). Employees looked up the purchases of celebrities such as Kanye West, and spied on their exes and romantic partners (Evans, 2021).

Any customer care representative could during this time check virtually any customer's purchasing history at any time (Evans, 2021). Because of how widely these access rights were dispersed, it was simple for staff to abuse their authority to snoop on Amazon customers.

A hacker going by the handle #0x2Taylor claimed on Twitter in July 2016 to have accessed an Amazon server and stolen the personal data of more than 80,000 Kindle customers (Ehrenkranz, 2016). If Amazon would not pay him $700, he threatened to disclose the information. He published this information online since Amazon failed to compensate him (Heiligenstein, 2022).

Amazon refuted claims that its systems had been compromised, saying, "We have determined that this material did not come from Amazon's computers and that the accounts in issue are not authentic Amazon customer accounts" (Heiligenstein, 2022). It's difficult to say for certain if Amazon was genuinely compromised in this scenario.

2017

Employees at Amazon found a stockpile of American Express payment card data on the company's internal network in May 2017 (Evans, 2021). This credit card information was widely accessible to Amazon workers for at least a few months. It is unknown whether this publicly accessible data was misused when it was out in the open because their audit logs only dated back 90 days.

2018

A third-party business was selling Amazon user data to unaffiliated vendors in May 2018, according to Amazon (Evans, 2021). For many years, Amazon provided vendors with extensive access to customer information, including name and address (Evans, 2021). This information was gathered in bulk by AMZReview, who linked it to other consumer data exposed in prior breaches. Information on up to 16 million Amazon customers was available through AMZReview. However, there was a far greater issue: Amazon discovered that more than half of third-party developers were breaking the terms of service, and some third-party businesses had access to up to a billion orders.

Amazon responded by tightening its regulations on user data. However, they kept their comments regarding the data loss under wraps. A spokeswoman for Amazon asserted that "There was not a data leak" in answer to questions from Wired reporters, but had "no comment" when asked how many customers' data had been improperly collected by other firms (Evans, 2021).

The Wall Street Journal revealed in September 2018 that Amazon workers have been unethically providing consumer data in return for kickbacks (Francisco, 2018). Chinese dealers apparently purchased this data from employees in both China and the United States for rates between $80 and $2,000. Internal metrics and private information, such as reviewers' email addresses, were both included in the data.

Similar conduct was discovered in May 2018 by Amazon's security team, which discovered that Amazon workers in China had been evading security measures, seizing control of customers' accounts, and erasing user reviews (Reed, 2021). Given that many of these workers seem to have acted alone, these two occurrences could not have been directly connected. But Amazon has always struggled with internal challenges of this nature.

In November 2018, Amazon revealed a significant data breach, including consumer names and email addresses only two days before Black Friday (Brignall, 2018). The business claimed that it contacted the affected people but withheld information about the breach's scope, which it portrayed as a technical error that resulted in the unintentional publication of individuals' private information on the website.

Amazon's security division learned in November 2018 that Krasr, a third-party merchant, had paid around $160,000 in bribes to Amazon personnel (Evans, 2021). They sabotaged Krasr's rivals on Amazon's marketplace in return. Seven employees who had stolen money from Krasr were found and fired by Amazon (Evans, 2021). Although they forwarded Krasr to the FBI, it doesn't seem like its owner has been detained or accused with any crimes.

2020

Amazon discovered a group of workers exchanging private customer information with other parties in January 2020 (Whittaker, 2020). It's unclear exactly how many client phone numbers and email addresses were made public. Amazon dismissed the affected employees as a result. These two events may or may not have been related, but Amazon has not provided any more information.

Six persons were charged in September 2020 by a grand jury in Washington with paying Amazon workers to give them an unfair edge in Amazon's third-party marketplace (Six Indicted in Connection with Multi-Million Dollar Scheme to Bribe Amazon Employees and Contractors, 2020). Three of the six defendants had their own items for sale, and all six had offered advice to Amazon sellers. These vendors attacked other sellers, illegally collected consumer data, and reinstated product listings that Amazon had previously removed through bribery and fraud.

Disgruntled Amazon staff members leaked a lot of Amazon customers' email addresses to third parties willingly for the second time in 2020 (Sharma, 2020). The workers in charge of the insider breach were let go. Although Amazon contacted any consumers whose email addresses may have been sent to a third party directly, it is unclear exactly how many customers were affected by the issue.

As illustrated, Amazon frequently deals with internal threats. Employees at Amazon have repeatedly divulged confidential information to outside parties, including customer data.

2021

Amazon was penalised 746 million euros in July 2021 by the Luxembourg National Commission for Data Protection for allegedly breaking the General Data Protection Regulation of the European Union (GDPR). The Commission claims that Amazon violated the GDPR's legal requirements by improperly handling personal data.

Amazon responded by claiming they will contest the penalties since there had been "no data breach" and that it was "without merit."

June 2022

Paige Thompson, a former employee of Amazon, was found guilty in June 2022 for her participation in the 2019 Capital One hack. Thompson took advantage of her understanding of cloud server vulnerabilities at Capital One and more than 30 other firms while working for Amazon Web services. In total, Thompson took the names, dates of birth, and social security numbers of more than 100 million people.

During the trial, the defense painted Thompson as an ethical hacker who wanted to alert businesses to security flaws before "bad actors" could take advantage of them. The U.S. Department of Justice disagreed, pointing out that Thompson did not inform the organizations whose data she compromised, boasted about the incident on hacker forums while using an alias, and made money off the breach by installing crypto mining software on many of the servers she compromised. In his closing remarks, assistant U.S. attorney Andrew Friedman stated that "she wanted data, she wanted money, and she wanted to brag."

A Seattle jury found Thompson guilty of wire fraud, five counts of unauthorised access to a protected computer, and destroying a protected computer after deliberating for 10 hours. She was found not guilty of aggravated identity theft and access device fraud by the jury. The maximum sentence for Thompson is 45 years in prison.

It appears that Capital One was not totally blameless in the event. The office of the Comptroller of Currency penalised Capital One $80 million for having lax security procedures, and the business also agreed to pay a $190 million settlement in a class action lawsuit.

Conclusion

In this section, two of the largest data breaches have been examined. There have been many other data breaches of small and large scale in companies such as Equifax, Yahoo, LinkedIn, Marriott International, Adult Friend Finder, MySpace, NetEase, Adobe, Wonga Loans, Quora, and Vision Direct, to name a few.

A lot can be learned from these examples of breaches of personal data from these big companies. Both the European Union and the state of California had implemented extensive new data privacy legislation in order to stop abuses like these. From South Dakota, Committee chair John Thune claimed that Congress was now prepared to draught its own regulations (Evans, 2021). The issue of whether a federal statute is required to safeguard customers' privacy has a clear answer, he insisted; what form will that law take is the question (Evans, 2021).

References

Archibong, I. (2018, August 22). An Update on Our App Investigation. Meta. https://about.fb.com/news/2018/08/update-on-app-investigation/

Arkose Labs. (2020, April 28). Arkose Labs Reveals 20% Spike in Fraud as Digital Behavior Shifts During COVID-19. GlobeNewswire News Room. https://www.globenewswire.com/news-release/2020/04/28/2023282/0/en/Arkose-Labs-Reveals-20-Spike-in-Fraud-as-Digital-Behavior-Shifts-During-COVID-19.html

Brignall, M. (2018, November 21). Amazon hit with major data breach days before Black Friday. The Guardian. https://www.theguardian.com/technology/2018/nov/21/amazon-hit-with-major-data-breach-days-before-black-friday

Cadwalladr, C., & Graham-Harrison, E. (2018, March 17). Revealed: 50 million Facebook profiles harvested for Cambridge Analytica in major data breach. The Guardian. https://www.theguardian.com/news/2018/mar/17/cambridge-analytica-facebook-influence-us-election

Confessore, N. (2018, April 4). Cambridge Analytica and Facebook: The Scandal and the Fallout So Far. The New York Times. https://www.nytimes.com/2018/04/04/us/politics/cambridge-analytica-scandal-fallout.html

Confessore, N., & Rosenberg, M. (2018, March 28). Spy Contractor's Idea Helped Cambridge Analytica Harvest Facebook Data. The New York Times. https://www.nytimes.com/2018/03/27/us/cambridge-analytica-palantir.html

Egan, E. (2018, May 1). Getting Feedback on New Tools to Protect People's Privacy. Meta. https://about.fb.com/news/2018/05/clear-history-2/

Ehrenkranz, M. (2016, July). A Hacker Claims to Have Leaked 80,000 Amazon Users' Passwords and Personal Information. Mic. https://www.mic.com/articles/148207/a-hacker-claims-to-have-leaked-80-000-amazon-users-passwords-and-personal-information

Evans, W. (2021, November 18). Amazon's Dark Secret: It Has Failed to Protect Your Data. Wired. https://www.wired.com/story/amazon-failed-to-protect-your-data-investigation/

Francisco, J. E. in H. K. and L. S. and R. M. in S. (2018). Amazon Investigates Employees Leaking Data for Bribes. WSJ. https://www.wsj.com/articles/amazon-investigates-employees-leaking-data-for-bribes-1537106401

Grewal, P. (2018, March 17). Suspending Cambridge Analytica and SCL Group From Facebook. Meta. https://about.fb.com/news/2018/03/suspending-cambridge-analytica/

Hakim, D., & Rosenberg, M. (2018, March 17). Data Firm Tied to Trump Campaign Talked Business With Russians. The New York Times. https://www.nytimes.com/2018/03/17/us/politics/cambridge-analytica-russia.html

Heiligenstein, M. X. (2022, June 22). Amazon Data Breaches: Full Timeline Through 2022. Firewall Times. https://firewalltimes.com/amazon-data-breach-timeline/

Hsu, T. (2018, March 21). For Many Facebook Users, a 'Last Straw' That Led Them to Quit. The New York Times. https://www.nytimes.com/2018/03/21/technology/users-abandon-facebook.html

Kang, C., & Frenkel, S. (2018, April 4). Facebook Says Cambridge Analytica Harvested Data of Up to 87 Million Users. The New York Times. https://www.nytimes.com/2018/04/04/technology/mark-zuckerberg-testify-congress.html

Kang, C., & Roose, K. (2018, April 11). Zuckerberg Faces Hostile Congress as Calls for Regulation Mount. The New York Times. https://www.nytimes.com/2018/04/11/business/zuckerberg-facebook-congress.html

Kumar, M. (2014, December 27). Hackers leak 13,000 Passwords Of Amazon, Walmart and Brazzers Users. The Hacker News. https://thehackernews.com/2014/12/password-hacking-data-breach.html

Mac, R. (2019, February). Former Facebook Employees Say The Company's Recent Prioritization Of Privacy Is All About Optics. BuzzFeed News. https://www.buzzfeednews.com/article/ryanmac/facebook-privacy-optics-clear-history-zuckerberg

Office of the Privacy Commissioner of Canada. (2018, October 29). What you need to know about mandatory reporting of breaches of security safeguards. Office of the Privacy Commissioner of Canada. https://www.priv.gc.ca/en/privacy-topics/business-privacy/safeguards-and-breaches/privacy-breaches/respond-to-a-privacy-breach-at-your-business/gd_pb_201810/

Reed, C. (2021, August 2). Internal Threats: Everything You Need to Know. Firewall Times. https://firewalltimes.com/internal-threats/

Roose, K., & Kang, C. (2018, April 11). Mark Zuckerberg Testifies on Facebook Before Skeptical Lawmakers. The New York Times. https://www.nytimes.com/2018/04/10/us/politics/zuckerberg-facebook-senate-hearing.html

Rosenberg, M. (2018a, March 20). Cambridge Analytica Suspends C.E.O. Amid Facebook Data Scandal. The New York Times. https://www.nytimes.com/2018/03/20/world/europe/cambridge-analytica-ceo-suspended.html

Rosenberg, M. (2018b, March 23). Bolton Was Early Beneficiary of Cambridge Analytica's Facebook Data. The New York Times. https://www.nytimes.com/2018/03/23/us/politics/bolton-cambridge-analyticas-facebook-data.html

Rosenberg, M., Confessore, N., & Cadwalladr, C. (2018a, March 17). How Trump Consultants Exploited the Facebook Data of Millions. The New York Times. https://www.nytimes.com/2018/03/17/us/politics/cambridge-analytica-trump-campaign.html

Rosenberg, M., Confessore, N., & Cadwalladr, C. (2018b, March 17). How Trump Consultants Exploited the Facebook Data of Millions. The New York Times. https://www.nytimes.com/2018/03/17/us/politics/cambridge-analytica-trump-campaign.html

Rosenberg, M., & Dance, G. J. X. (2018, April 8). 'You Are the Product': Targeted by Cambridge Analytica on Facebook. The New York Times. https://www.nytimes.com/2018/04/08/us/facebook-users-data-harvested-cambridge-analytica.html

Rosenberg, M., & Frenkel, S. (2018, March 18). Facebook's Role in Data Misuse Sets Off Storms on Two Continents. The New York Times. https://www.nytimes.com/2018/03/18/us/cambridge-analytica-facebook-privacy-data.html

Sharma, A. (2020). Amazon sacks insiders over data leak, alerts customers. BleepingComputer. https://www.bleepingcomputer.com/news/security/amazon-sacks-insiders-over-data-leak-alerts-customers/

Six indicted in connection with multi-million dollar scheme to bribe Amazon employees and contractors. (2020, September 18). https://www.justice.gov/usao-wdwa/pr/six-indicted-connection-multi-million-dollar-scheme-bribe-amazon-employees-and

Smith, D. (2019, March 8). Elizabeth Warren vows to break up Amazon, Facebook and Google if elected president. The Guardian. https://www.theguardian.com/us-news/2019/mar/08/elizabeth-warren-amazon-facebook-google-big-tech-break-up-blogpost

Whittaker, Z. (2020). Amazon fires employees for leaking customer email addresses and phone numbers | TechCrunch. https://techcrunch.com/2020/01/10/amazon-employees-email-address/

Wong, J. C. (2019, March 18). The Cambridge Analytica scandal changed the world – but it didn't change Facebook. The Guardian. https://www.theguardian.com/technology/2019/mar/17/the-cambridge-analytica-scandal-changed-the-world-but-it-didnt-change-facebook

PRIVACY POLICIES

By Christina Nguyen

A Primer To Algorithmic Accountability And North American Legal Implications

When we consider the question of algorithmic accountability, and think about and how we can make artificial intelligence systems work for us rather than against us, one of the major issues that come up for discussion is discrimination and categorization. Many people have written about this and given explanations of where discrimination comes from; one of the reasons presented is that learning algorithms often collect historical data, and therefore are projecting inequalities from the past into the future in the eventual model. For example, a learning model using data about the usage of Twitter in 2018-2020 may be used to predict how many people will be using Twitter in 2022-2024. Unfortunately, there are many variables that are not considered in the data, such as Elon Musk's acquisition of the Twitter company, simply because this does not exist in the historical data collection. Twitter may very well have no users at all by 2024, or become a small den of extremist conversation (Benton et al. 2022). The historical data is also often linked to "protected attributes," an American legal term (created prior of the popularized usage of algorithms) that refers to characteristics such as gender, income, religion, and age. These attributes have historically been used by some humans as a means of discriminating against other humans; thus the original coinage in the USA was as a special category for people qualified for exceptional protection under the law. Note also that the terms of "protected group" and "protected classes" are frequently used in the USA, while Canada often uses the term "prohibited grounds of discrimination (motif de distinction illicite)" ("Loi Canadienne Sur Les Droits de La Personne" n.d.). Alas, with the growing use of classification algorithms in the digital landscape with many legal grey areas, algorithms are not just grouping us according to these protected attributes, they are also grouping us in harmful groups outside of protected attributes.

Harmful Discrimination Outside Of Protected Attributes

A sample case follows of harmful groupings outside of protected attributes. A person applies to a job online, using their personal computer. The company looking to hire them now has the person's IP address from a specific geographical region, and in that case the applicant may be more likely to be rejected because they live in a low-income and/or stigmatized area of the city. This case is interesting because while "geographic area" is an attribute which an algorithm can identify and classify, it is not yet an attribute that is protected under the laws enforced by the U.S. Equal Employment Opportunity Commission (U.S. Equal Employment Opportunity Commission n.d.), yet it can still be used to discriminate against an individual. In other words, it is entirely the case that the classification algorithms are grouping us in such groups that hold us back with no formally legal ways of recourse. Other potentially unfair classes noted by the literature includes: predicting educational levels, predicting region of habitation by studying dialect, and predicting body type (shape) to better tailor fashion advertisements or content recommendations (Lydia Kollyri 2021).

The American non-discrimination law, previously alluded to, contains the descriptions of the protected attributes. To be precise, outside of these protected classes of people, we have two other algorithmic groups that may be created by algorithms. In the literature, they are referred to as the "non-protected" and "incomprehensible" groups or ways of arriving at decisions (Mittelstadt et al. 2016a). In the former case, we have cases like "I'm being grouped as a person who prefers to wear loafers, and am disproportionately targeted by loafer ads; I'm being grouped as a Minecraft gamer; I'm being grouped an person who needs to get out into nature more;" these are legitimate groups and possibly unfair/fair conclusions to reach, but they do not currently have any protection.

On the second case, we have algorithmic groups that are unexplainable and completely opaque in terms of rationale; we do not even have human language to describe what is going on or how people are being grouped by the computer; these decisions are nearly black-boxes (Mittelstadt et al. 2016a). As Iyer et al. observe about deep neural networks particularly:

Developing methods to enable autonomous agents to be transparent [about their models] is very challenging, because ease of transparency seems to be inversely proportional to agent sophistication. Recently Deep Neural Networks (DNNs) have allowed agents to reach almost human performance in multiple tasks such as computer vision, natural language processing and control tasks. More specifically, recent work has found outstanding performances of deep reinforcement learning (DRL) models on Atari 2600 games, by using only raw pixels to make decisions. However, DNNs are extremely opaque i.e., they cannot produce human understandable accounts [my emphasis] of their reasoning processes or explanations. (Iyer et al. 2018)

Yet these classifications, which are little more than electronic signals and beeps with no human-understanding explanations, are being used to make important influential decisions in the machines controlling our lives. In these cases, specifically, the conversation around creating possible legal protection (i.e. adding more protected classes) for vulnerable groups is rendered that much more impossible; if there is no term for a social concept to describe what is going on, then there can be no legal protection or moral understanding of how things came to be so. And thus there can also be no legal repercussions of regulation. From that implication, no user, no matter how tech-savvy or knowledgeable, can truly consent to the sharing of their own data if they do not even understand how the data is being used to make decisions, beyond some generic "computer signal" explanation. Mitterlstadt et al. summarize it as:

> **The rationale of an algorithm can in contrast be incomprehensible to humans, rendering the legitimacy of decisions difficult to challenge. Under these conditions, decision-making is poorly transparent. Rubel and Jones (2014) argue that the failure to render the processing logic comprehensible to data subject's disrespects their agency [...] Meaningful consent to data-processing is not possible when opacity precludes risk assessment.**

(Mittelstadt et al. 2016b)

The right to understand how an algorithmic decision is made, and weaknesses in deep learning

There is already a case to be made that the ability to question an AI system's reasoning processes is a fundamental legal right. As Rodrigues writes, though, even that is not a presupposition for correctness: "transparency has its limitations and is often viewed as inadequate and limited. For example, as Vaccaro and Karahalios point out, 'Even when machine learning decisions can be explained, decision-subjects may not agree with the outcome'" (Rodrigues 2020). In the situations of no transparency, such as deep learning, incomprehensible grouping will be cast under more scrutiny than ever before. The European Union, for example, may mandate that businesses be able to provide users with an explanation for decisions that automated systems arrive at (Mark MacCarthy and Kenneth Propp 2021; Tambiama n.d.). Even for systems that appear to be relatively simple at first glance, such as the apps and websites that use deep learning to serve ads or recommend songs, this might be impossible. These services are run by computers that have written their own programmes in ways we cannot comprehend. Even these applications' developers themselves are unable to fully explain their behavior (Iyer et al. 2018; Mittelstadt et al. 2016a).

Such deep learning neural network systems cannot implement interventions ('What if we do X?') or counterfactuals ('What if, instead of X, we had done Y?') because they lack internal models or representations out of their frames of context. To determine the connection between a medication and a patient's prognosis, they can learn historical patient treatment and outcome data; for example, if drug A was used on a patient with diabetes, it could help them better regulate their X hormone. They are unable to undertake interventions, however, by speculating on what may occur if a component of the recommended course of therapy or a drug's active ingredients were changed; for example, if drug B was used instead of drug A, what would happen differently? In the same vein, they are also unable to use counterfactual reasoning to determine what would, should, or could have occurred in the past if alternative choices had been made or a different course of therapy had been used. In terms of what is known as artificial general intelligence, or AGI, or the capacity to match or outperform human intellect across several types of cognitive task, they are thus a long way from being intelligent on par with humans, and potentially are missing fairness because they are not able to contemplate other situations with other variables

Deep learning weak AI systems are notoriously difficult to ensure morality. These issues are primarily brought on by the internal, hidden layers of statistical neuron logic's lack of transparency. In other words, to understand how a deep neural network functions, you can not only peek inside of it. The action of thousands of artificial neurons, organised into dozens or even hundreds of highly interconnected layers, contains the reasoning of a network ("(17) But What Is a Neural Network? | Chapter 1, Deep Learning - YouTube" n.d.). Each of the neurons in the first layer receives an input, such as the intensity of a pixel in an image, and then computes before producing a new signal. The neurons in the subsequent layer get these outputs through a complicated web of connections, and so on, until an overall output is created. Additionally, a procedure called back-propagation modifies the calculations made by individual neurons in a way that enables the network to learn to produce a particular output ("(17) But What Is a Neural Network? | Chapter 1, Deep Learning - YouTube" n.d.). While much research has been made in recent years to gain an insight into how the neurons work and how back-propagation works, however, a lot is still lacking. Higher-level pattern recognition and complicated decision-making depend on the interaction of calculations inside a deep neural network, but those calculations are a maze of mathematical functions and variables. You might be able to understand it if you had a very modest neural network. But when it grows to be very big, with thousands of units per layer and perhaps hundreds of layers, it becomes very difficult to understand. And if the creator has such issues understanding the system, how can the average person, whose life is inherently shaped by the system, defend their rights to know how their information is being collected and used?

The code, learned rules, and underlying architectural designs of the systems that support their run-time activities are typically physically accessible to computer scientists. This is accomplished with the aid of tools like memory dumps and snapshots, which output a "snapshot" of the contents of the memory during programme execution. Other ways take advantage of complex development environments that can step through (line by line of code) and observe code execution, as well as the inputs, outputs, and activity of the program's functions and methods. On the other hand, there is no direct access to the logic of the taught statistical hidden layer nodes, or neurons, of a deep learning system. By giving the system extreme inputs to train it, such as blank images in the case of image recognition systems, they must be estimated or speculated. For other reasons, epistemic opacity is a natural result of cognitive overload, and systems may be designed to be "simplified" to black boxes. Engineering requires the use of black boxes, which are by nature epistemically opaque. For example, a aerospace engineer does not always want to know about the forces holding an atom together, while he is building a component. Thus, engineering black box abstraction is also a result of design, benefiting from "divide and conquer" modularity and reducing conceptual clutter.

The Non-Discrimination Law

Why was the non-discrimination law (NDL) created in the first place, and is it still valid in light of the challenges we face today? Unfortunately, the definitions of "non-protected" and "incomprehensible" still need to be created, despite the fact that the anti-discrimination law should apply in circumstances when there are no "protected classes" ("The Ontario Human Rights Code | Ontario Human Rights Commission" n.d.). Your independence and self-sufficiency are the cornerstones of the law, according to this essential premise. You should be able to pursue an education, a fulfilling calling in life and to be your own person and make your own success in life (in other words, a quasi-meritocracy). Additionally, you ought to have access to housing, food, and medical care. You can see what is necessary to be a self-sufficient member of society if you look at those industries. Because we humans have used the "protected attributes" to discriminate against people and deny them access to the things (sectors) to which they are legally entitled, the law protects them.

The discrimination outcome is the same even though the algorithms are using criteria that were not in place when the NDL was first created ("A History of the Employment Non-Discrimination Act - Center for American Progress" n.d.). It is founded on unfair traits that we often do not actively pursue; they are things that are bestowed onto you without your understanding (e.g. as mentioned before, it could be your height, your geographical area, the color of your eyes, and what types of shoes you like to wear on a day-to-day basis). We need to rethink and update the NDL because an action can be discriminatory even if it is not directed at a protected class.

In Canada, for example, we have the Canadian Human Rights Act that works similarly, to protect people who are employed or receive services from the federal government, First Nations governments, or private companies that are regulated by the federal government ("RSC 1985, c H-6 | Canadian Human Rights Act | CanLII" n.d.). This includes financial institutions, transportation firms, media outlets, and telecom firms.

Changing Our Perception Of The NDL To See The Whole

The term "artificial immutability" is derived from the notion that certain protected characteristics, such as age and others, are protected because you had no control over their acquisition, like the previously mentioned eye color. The law is only concerned with things that you do (your deeds), not with things that are out of your control. As a result, you start to believe that immutable qualities are something you cannot choose but rather were given to you. Thus, "artificial immutability" refers to the notion that algorithms categorize you into fictitious groups that appear to be immutable; they assign you a value that you cannot change, even if it is incorrect (which may not be the case). You might remark, "Oh, I cannot hire you because you are five foot two inches tall," in the conventional, non-AI meaning. That is a fundamentally unchangeable quality. It implies that the standards set for me are unchangeable and unalterable, and often, that is a problem. Now, in the AI, digital data-gathering sense, it may change to be "Oh, I cannot hire you because you have been observed buying clothing online for someone who is five foot two inches tall, and we think that you are that height, and we cannot hire someone that short." Due to artificially immutable qualities like that height, and indicators of that height, algorithms mimic these pre-existing issues. It is all about a quality of you that you cannot alter, being used to deny you some service.

Immutability and reasoning: what makes good transparency?

Why is anything unchangeable? How can we demonstrate that, even if we wanted to, it is something that cannot be changed? The first definition is that it might be that the decision criteria are too ambiguous, such as "Your geographic area is the reason you are not getting a loan," which is too ambiguous to give me a sense of what geographic area is good for getting a loan and does not explain why my geographic area is bad for getting that loan (Wachter n.d.). I cannot relocate far enough to qualify for a loan if I do not know where to go – is it because I live at the Jane and Finch intersection in Toronto, a historically crime-ridden area? Or is it because I am in the North York region in the city of Toronto, and need to move altogether out of North York (e.g. towards Etobicoke or Scarborough)? If I am unsure of what needs to change, how can I present myself in the best light? A lack of stability is the second definition. The requirements for an algorithm's decision-making may fluctuate; for example, one day you might need to be wearing blue jeans to get a loan, but the next you might need to be wearing dress pants. The loan applicant cannot prepare for or exert influence over the outcome because they cannot predict what the criteria will be on any given day. Involuntariness is the third definition, and once more, face recognition software measures something you cannot physically influence. The final definition, "social notion," refers to social groups for which there is neither a word nor a human knowledge of what those groups include. They are manufactured immutabilities since you are powerless to change them (Wachter n.d.).

The other thing that makes this so intriguing is that these qualities are constructed artificially by the companies that develop and use AI systems, and as a result, they inadvertently create their own problems. So in a sense, it is a question for regulators to ask themselves: "Should we be looking at this quality for regulation (i.e. turning it into a protected class), if people are basing their decisions on immutable attributes?" But we should also hold organizations partially accountable by asking them "why are you creating immutable attributes?" For example, it is possible that the Epic gaming company (the owners of Fortnite) created algorithms to target vulnerable populations (in this case, mostly children) with specific psychological characteristics to cause them to be addicted to the game. In a recent case, a Quebec Superior Court judge has authorized a class action lawsuit against Epic, to determine if they willingly targeted these qualities ("Quebec Class Action Alleging Fortnite Is Addictive Will Go Ahead, Judge Rules | CBC News" n.d.).

Both parties should be interested in finding a solution to this issue because it may have effects on both design and regulation. Why did the computer believe that the x electrical signal meant we should deny someone a loan is just something that is typically valuable or good for a corporation to know? This is not to argue that traits that cannot be changed are always undesirable. It just needs to be given some more careful thought.

Trust Is Hard When Decisions Are Opaque, And Grouping Seems Unfair

The use and deployment of computerised systems, including AI, is impacted by a critical issue that is at their core: trust. For instance, educational institutions are rapidly considering or are currently utilising the possibilities of AI, much like many other companies. We already know that user trust and the integrity of AI are strongly influenced by transparency. Users are more likely to view an algorithm as trustworthy and valuable when they believe it to be transparent, explicable, accountable, and fair. As a result, those in charge of implementing AI must be able to explain why it is necessary and give those who will be impacted a basic understanding of how it works. The absence of trust emphasises how important it is because it makes success with AI much more challenging to achieve. Failures in AI can reduce the value of interpersonal trust and absolve those responsible for its development and deployment of responsibility. In addition to having a negative effect on AI adoption, mistrust can lead to users ignoring the recommendations made by AI, returning to the use of human decision-making processes, for example.

This is demonstrated by the International Baccalaureate's recent decision to forecast final exam results for its students using artificial intelligence (AI) in the wake of cancelling in-person exams ("What Happens When AI Is Used to Set Grades?" n.d.). Particularly, issues with the method utilized to forecast pupils' grades were brought up. The opaqueness of the algorithm's operation was a major reason for skepticism. Teachers, parents, and students were all perplexed by how the formula determined grades, and some even questioned how the algorithm was created and tested.

Final exams were previously assessed and moderated by IBO-affiliated human markers, hence the method utilised to determine final scores diverged significantly from accepted standards and practises ("What Happens When AI Is Used to Set Grades?" n.d.). It became clear that the grading calculation was based on a student's assignment scores, teacher anticipated grades, and school context even if information regarding the exact workings of the algorithm was not made publicly available. Although it was agreed that school context was not based on the success of prior cohorts, there was a belief that a strong kid from a school that underperformed might be degraded by school environment. At lower levels, a constrictive environment was fostered by the deployment of an algorithm to anticipate grades. At both the individual and collective levels, a situation of frustration, rage, and mistrust developed in a very short period of time. Parents, educators, and students banded together in opposition, organising a collective action and voicing serious concerns about the algorithm's fairness, objectivity, and transparency (i.e. clear communication)("What Happens When AI Is Used to Set Grades?" n.d.).

When upper-level communication is opaque and an initiative's intended goal falls short of people's expectations, it may foster a climate of mistrust and cynicism. Details on the grading procedure for IB were not immediately clear. The openness and justice that the students expected from the system were not delivered. Safety, security/robustness, privacy, transparency and fairness, ethics and sustainability, and accountability are the six main factors that can cause mistrust in AI. In the IB case, it is evident that mistrust was mostly caused by a lack of openness and justice, particularly during a time when kids' education was severely disrupted and homeschooling and a lack of face-to-face instruction were the norm. Despite generally being thought of as a reliable company, confidence soon diminished.

A legitimacy gap occurred between how individuals believed IBO should behave, based on their global credibility and high education quality standards, and the actual actions taken by the firm. This discrepancy destabilized legitimacy, promoting values of deception and mistrust at lower levels.

A Pessimistic Ending

In sum, the unfettered continued use of opaque systems (deliberately or not), with little legal clarity, brings in an era of highly unethical uses of AI for us all. The basic right to understand how a decision is made is removed, and there is no clear idea of who is responsible for any potentially wrong decisions that the machine makes, even if the decision has terrible consequences for the individuals concerned. Real-life examples abound, and we need much more clarification before humans can trust the decisions made by algorithms.

References

"(17) But What Is a Neural Network? | Chapter 1, Deep Learning - YouTube." n.d. Accessed December 12, 2022. https://www.youtube.com/watch?v=aircAruvnKk&t=11s.

"A History of the Employment Non-Discrimination Act - Center for American Progress." n.d. Accessed December 5, 2022. https://www.americanprogress.org/article/a-history-of-the-employment-non-discrimination-act/.

Benton, Bond, Jin-A Choi, Yi Luo, and Keith Green. 2022. "Hate Speech Spikes on Twitter After Elon Musk Acquires the Platform." School of Communication and Media, Montclair State University, November. https://digitalcommons.montclair.edu/scom-facpubs/33.

Iyer, Rahul, Yuezhang Li, Huao Li, Michael Lewis, Ramitha Sundar, and Katia Sycara. 2018. "Transparency and Explanation in Deep Reinforcement Learning Neural Networks."

https://doi.org/10.1145/3278721.3278776.

"Loi Canadienne Sur Les Droits de La Personne." n.d. Accessed December 12, 2022. https://laws-lois.justice.gc.ca/fra/lois/h-6/page-1.html.

Lydia Kollyri. 2021. "De-Coding Instagram as a Spectacle: A Critical Algorithm Audit Analysis." Journal for Critical Media Inquiry, 103–24.

Mark MacCarthy, and Kenneth Propp. 2021. "Machines Learn That Brussels Writes the Rules: The EU's New AI Regulation." May 4, 2021. https://www.brookings.edu/blog/techtank/2021/05/04/machines-learn-that-brussels-writes-the-rules-the-eus-new-ai-regulation/.

Mittelstadt, Brent Daniel, Patrick Allo, Mariarosaria Taddeo, Sandra Wachter, and Luciano Floridi. 2016a. "The Ethics of Algorithms: Mapping the Debate." Http://Dx.Doi.Org/10.1177/2053951716679679 3 (2). https://doi.org/10.1177/2053951716679679.

"Quebec Class Action Alleging Fortnite Is Addictive Will Go Ahead, Judge Rules | CBC News." n.d. Accessed December 12, 2022. https://www.cbc.ca/news/canada/montreal/fortnite-class-action-1.6678687.

Rodrigues, Rowena. 2020. "Legal and Human Rights Issues of AI: Gaps, Challenges and Vulnerabilities." Journal of Responsible Technology 4 (December): 100005. https://doi.org/10.1016/J.JRT.2020.100005.

"RSC 1985, c H-6 | Canadian Human Rights Act | CanLII." n.d. Accessed December 5, 2022. https://www.canlii.org/en/ca/laws/stat/rsc-1985-c-h-6/latest/rsc-1985-c-h-6.html.

Tambiama, Madiega. n.d. "EU Guidelines on Ethics in Artificial Intelligence: Context and Implementation." Accessed December 12, 2022.

"The Ontario Human Rights Code | Ontario Human Rights Commission." n.d. Accessed December 5, 2022. https://www.ohrc.on.ca/en/ontario-human-rights-code.

U.S. Equal Employment Opportunity Commission. n.d. "Prohibited Employment Policies/Practices | U.S. Equal Employment Opportunity Commission." Accessed December 12, 2022. https://www.eeoc.gov/prohibited-employment-policiespractices.

Wachter, Sandra. n.d. "THE THEORY OF ARTIFICIAL IMMUTABILITY: PROTECTING ALGORITHMIC GROUPS UNDER ANTI-DISCRIMINATION LAW." Accessed December 5, 2022.

"What Happens When AI Is Used to Set Grades?" n.d. Accessed December 5, 2022. https://hbr.org/2020/08/what-happens-when-ai-is-used-to-set-grades.

META SCANNING PEOPLE'S FACES

By Muhammad Ans

One of the biggest concerns social media users have today revolves around corporations unnecessarily scanning our faces and most often so without our permission. This has caused many users around the world to close up their cameras, either by using a camera cover or simply by putting a piece of tape over their cameras in hopes of protecting their privacy. The process of scanning a user's face for a variety of purposes is known as facial recognition or facial scanning (Liu et al., 2021). The pervasive use of facial recognition technologies is extremely complex. On one side, there are serious ethical concerns about compromising the public's privacy (Liu et al., 2021). However, facial recognition technologies also provide benefits to the public as they allow for increased security and can be used to locate missing persons (Liu et al., 2021). One of the largest corporations to employ this strategy is Meta, formerly known as Facebook. In a recent press release, Meta claims that they aim to use their facial recognition software to verify the age of their Instagram users (Sato, 2022). The social media giant claimed that they aim to use this software if there arises a suspicion that the user may be under the age of 18 (Sato, 2022). In the future, Meta aims to use this technology in Facebook dating as well, to verify that users are being truthful about their age (Sato, 2022). If any suspicions arise, Meta asks users to upload a picture of their face, a selfie, and this is sent to a third-party company for verification. Meta has partnered with Yoti to carry out this verification procedure (Sato, 2022). This is where the concern comes in. How can users trust that pictures of their faces are appropriately being handled by a company that they have never heard of, especially given the uncertainty around cybersecurity as of late? However, Yoti states that its system is quite accurate. It identifies the faces of 13 to 17-year-olds as under 23 accurately about 99 percent of the time. At the same time, the system is not exactly perfect. Data collected by Yoti states that its accuracy is worse for females and people with a darker complexion (Yoti, 2022). This has caused many to flag concerns over how facial recognition software may perform differently, or have a bias toward people of different races, ages, and/or gender (Lunter, 2020).

Before moving further, it is important to examine in detail what exactly facial recognition technologies are. In a nutshell, facial recognition technologies hereafter referred to as FRTs, are a form of biometric data collection tools that use matching patterns to identify individuals based on their facial characteristics (Liu et al., 2021). FRTs can match the image of a human face against a database of faces to verify one's identity. These systems have increasingly become popular to authenticate users through ID verification. FRTs can be found in shopping centers around the world and can be used to log into social media and verify one's identity at financial institutions. The emergence of FRTs dates back to 1937 when Woodrow W. Bledsoe used a software known as RAND to classify photos of human faces (Sullivan, 2021). Since then, FRTs have taken the world by storm, engaging in all aspects of human lives and vowing to make our lives easier (Sullivan, 2021). The use of FRTs has dramatically improved the intelligence of many businesses. This is mainly due to the fact that the human face is rich in features and as a result, is an excellent form of identification. However, as mentioned, there exists a lot of hesitation around the use of FRTs due to cited privacy concerns.

Shifting back to the social media giant Meta, it continues to fall under scrutiny for its use of facial recognition technology. Let us examine the evolution of Meta using these technologies. In 2011, then social media company Facebook announced that it would be offering facial recognition services to all its users. Through the use of the widely used 'tag feature', Facebook possessed the ability to automatically identify people in a photograph, given that the user has a Facebook account. Due to the widespread concerns by users worldwide surrounding privacy, a complaint was filed with the Federal Trade Commission of the United States. Before ultimately admitting to its faults, Facebook denied allegations surrounding the violation of privacy laws. Facebook admitting fault was extremely alarming as the company stored biometric data about its users and often distributed this data to third-party sources, all without the consent of its users (Heilweil, 2021).

In November 2021, Meta announced that it will be permanently suspending its facial recognition technology and thereby deleting approximately 1 billion faces currently stored in its database ('An Update on Our Use of Face Recognition', 2021). A statement released by Jerome Pesenti, the VP of Artificial Intelligence at Meta stated that this decision stems from the unease surrounding privacy concerns of facial recognition technologies ('An Update on Our Use of Face Recognition', 2021). However, he continued to outline the benefits that such technologies possess to everyday human endeavors. Although Facebook is eliminating facial recognition technology, Meta is not. Such services may show up elsewhere in the Metaverse (Heilweil, 2021).

Early this year, the state of Texas filed a lawsuit against Meta claiming illegal use of facial recognition software at the expense of the privacy of the public (Granitz, 2022). Attorney General Plaxton claimed that the company collected facial recognition data without users' consent and shared it with third-party companies and additionally, failed to destroy the data promptly. By using the 'tag feature' Facebook illegally linked a photo posted to a person's profile. As a response to this, Meta claimed that these claims are without merit (Granitz, 2022). However, they suspended their 'tag feature' by citing reasons involving societal concerns. Meta also cited a lack of regulations surrounding their alleged violation of privacy rules (Granitz, 2022). This again goes to show the privacy concerns centered around the use of facial recognition and the rather lack of regulations to control such processes.

Even though facial recognition is commonly viewed from a negative lens, this technology still possesses certain benefits for society. For example, facial recognition software can identify if someone is impersonating another individual and possibly put a stop to identity theft before further consequences arrive to the victim (Gargaro, 2022). Facial recognition also possesses a multitude of benefits in the realm of cyber security (Gargaro, 2022). With facial scans, social media users can ditch the use of PINs and passwords and move on to facial recognition (Gargaro, 2022). Alternatively, facial recognition can be used as a means of multifactor authentication to provide further security for users (Gargaro, 2022). Facial recognition technology also presents a possibility to make everyday human endeavors more efficient. Shopping centers can ditch the traditional use of credit cards and cash and simply use facial recognition and charge the customer to their account (Gargaro, 2022). This technology can also allow employees to simply clock in and out without the use of any key cards. All these are uses that can drastically reduce human touchpoints and this is extremely important to reduce the transmission of diseases, especially in a pandemic-riddled world. The greatest benefits of facial recognition exist in the surveillance and protection of citizens (Gargaro, 2022). Facial recognition can be and has been implemented as a measure to combat the recent increases in shoplifting. Law enforcement agencies can easily identify perpetrators by using surveillance cameras and matching images with a facial database. Similar processes can be implemented to improve security measures in banks and airports.

By now, facial recognition has become extremely common in our society. Countries around the world have started using facial recognition for more than just verifying users' age. In China, users can opt to use facial recognition to make purchases or even use the bathroom. However, the problem of bias becomes a major problem in the fact that law enforcement agencies around the world have employed this software for national security purposes. For example, it is estimated that the US government has facial recognition data on about half of the country's population (Lunter, 2020). If biased data collected by facial recognition services are used by government agencies, it could have severe implications on citizens' lives. Since facial recognition software presents a bias towards people with darker complexions, there may be a possibility that the use of this software by law enforcement agencies may make people of color more prone to be falsely accused of a crime (Lunter, 2020).

Now that we have examined the concerns surrounding the use of these software, let us examine what is currently being done to mitigate these issues. It has been revealed that companies currently do not have a solution to this problem. This is largely because companies do not currently have a benchmark to judge the accuracy of their software (Vincent, 2018). Most companies currently, when contacted to comment on this bias, refused to offer any details on how they plan to mitigate this issue (Vincent, 2018). However, most state that a benchmark must be implemented (Vincent, 2018). This is extremely alarming as the companies responsible for creating these software currently do not have a way to resolve this issue.

Privacy concerns are one of the major deterrents to facial recognition technologies. This was recently outlined by the FRT company Clearview (Klar, 2020). It was noted that Clearview was extracting images posted on Twitter and analyzing them using their software. However, once the news broke, Twitter demanded that Clearview immediately stop collecting such images from its platform (Klar, 2020). Clearview cited the recent success of their technologies as it has helped law enforcement agencies in identifying criminals across the US (Klar, 2020). This goes to show the lack of laws and regulations surrounding the use of facial recognition technologies and how this can breach the privacy of social media users worldwide. As stated, concerns surrounding the use of facial recognition and subsequent data storage are extremely widespread. A recent study demonstrated that facial recognition technologies are accurately able to predict a person's political orientation using natural facial images (Kosinski, 2021). A facial recognition algorithm utilized by the study aimed to correctly predict the political affiliation of almost 1.1 million participants (Kosinski, 2021). The technology used was accurately able to predict participants' political affiliation 72% of the time (Kosinski, 2021). Matches were made by comparing novel faces to faces with known political orientations. This is extremely alarming as the political affiliation of a user is sensitive information, something that most users would like to guard against the public. In certain unfortunate cases, one's political affiliation can lead one to be a victim of violent attacks. In addition to this, facial footprints of the public are easily accessible and due to this, software that can determine one's political affiliation may also be available to the public. This is a cause for concern because as stated, one's political affiliation is sensitive information. Looking forward to the future and further developments in facial recognition technology, we can only imagine that if facial recognition software can predict our extremely personal attributes such as sexual orientation, personality, or even private thoughts, our privacy is at a huge risk. The widespread use of facial recognition technologies is of great concern and can have catastrophic outcomes. Especially given that there continues to be little emphasis on regulations surrounding this issue (Almeida et al., 2022). Not only can this jeopardize the safety and privacy of the public, but can also negatively impact the development of facial recognition technologies (Almeida et al., 2022). Given the rapid development of facial recognition technology in the United States and North America, it is alarming that there is less emphasis on rules and regulations surrounding data and privacy in comparison to the European Union (EU) (Almeida et al., 2022).

As mentioned, in the face of the many negatives brought on by the excessive use of facial recognition technologies, it is hard to overlook the benefits it possesses. Technology, more specifically technological innovation continues to streamline every aspect of our lives. As technology innovates, it allows the rest of the world to follow suit. A study conducted by Liu and colleagues in China has stated that although the face of human beings continues to be examined in a social context, technology has given it a new meaning through innovation (Liu et al., 2021). Essentially, with the emergence of face recognition technologies, the face of human beings is increasingly being used to make our lives easier. This study surveyed the perception of approximately 500 users toward the use of facial recognition technologies in their daily lives. Although users cited certain privacy concerns due to the risk of their private information being disclosed, they were willing to provide this information in exchange for services and applications they need (Liu et al., 2021). In addition to this, it was found that users believe that facial recognition platforms do have the ability to create secure conditions but this claim was not widespread (Liu et al., 2021). From these findings, it can be gathered that users acknowledge the benefit of facial recognition technologies. However, for widespread usage, it is of the utmost importance that companies and governments tackle the concerns surrounding privacy in an effective and timely manner. As mentioned in the study, trust plays a vital role in the willingness of users to interact with any aspect of technology. Once users can confidently say that their privacy is not at risk while using facial recognition technologies, the reluctance around this new era of technology is bound to decrease (Liu et al., 2021). Another similar benefit offered by facial technologies revolves around finding missing people (Gargaro, 2022). Using live camera feeds, law enforcement authorities can use their facial recognition database to locate missing people by responding to a 'ping' if there is a match. Similar processes can be used to locate the most wanted perpetrators (Gargaro, 2022). All in all, it is clear that despite the harm that facial recognition technologies possess to our society, it also comes with immense benefits that make our communities safer.

It was earlier discussed that facial recognition technologies may have a role to play in the field of medicine. This is usually in the case of disease diagnosis. In the last decade, research on the use of facial recognition technologies in diagnosing certain diseases has exploded (Qiang et al., 2022). It has been noted that diseases not only have structural abnormalities but only manifest themselves in facial characteristics as well. Due to this, research by Qiang and colleagues was conducted in 2022 to test the efficacy of facial recognition technologies in accurately diagnosing diseases. The results of the study found that in comparison to traditionally used diagnostic tools, the use of facial recognition technologies was more accurate in diagnosing certain diseases (Qiang et al., 2022). This accuracy lies in the objective, comprehensive, and largely informative data that facial recognition technologies provide for further analysis and subsequent diagnosis (Qiang et al., 2022). The accuracy of facial recognition technologies was specifically observed in the diagnosis of endocrine, metabolic, genetic, chromosomal, neuromuscular, and acute and severe illnesses (Qiang et al., 2022). This again outlines another beneficial aspect of facial recognition technologies and further extends the need for the public's trust in such technologies so they can be further developed and deployed. Although the use of facial recognition technologies may seem beneficial based on the above research, ethical concerns continue to plague the use of such technologies in healthcare. This is because privacy and ethical concerns are even more pronounced in healthcare as sensitive information about patients may be at risk. For example, a tech start-up company known as Lapetus has partnered up with US insurer Legal & General America to offer life insurance quotes using facial recognition technologies (Facial Recognition Is Already Here, 2019). Essentially, Lapetus aims to measure the characteristics of a person such as their body mass index (BMI), age, gender, and any possible diseases (Facial Recognition Is Already Here, 2019). Although this may seem unique and beneficial, this can be extremely unethical and discriminatory. As mentioned earlier, facial recognition technology performs poorly when it comes to people of color and women. Therefore, using this technology to offer life insurance quotes to people from different ethnicities may provide information that does not accurately represent the subject's health condition (Lunter, 2020).

In addition to the use of facial recognition technologies in the fields of social media and healthcare, a very unlikely contender for the use of facial recognition technologies is the automotive industry. Although this may seem unlikely, the use of such technologies in vehicles may cut down on the increasing number of car thefts and insurance fraud (Facial Recognition Is Already Here, 2019). The American automotive manufacturer Ford has partnered with Intel to develop facial recognition technologies that can detect the primary and other authorized drivers. Without this verification, the vehicle will not start, thereby decreasing the rate of car theft. In addition to theft, facial recognition services in vehicles are also able to adjust the car according to driver preferences based on facial recognition alone (Facial Recognition Is Already Here, 2019). This was demonstrated by the Chrysler concept minivan which debuted in 2017. Travel insurance companies have also employed facial recognition technologies to bolster security at hotels, airports, and lounges (Facial Recognition Is Already Here, 2019).

Overall, it is clear that facial recognition technologies are not perfect. However, this is the case with any technology innovation and it is with time and further research that technologies are perfected. Regardless of this, the concerns cited against facial recognition technologies are of great concern as they breach the privacy of users worldwide. In addition to this, there exist certain ethical and discriminatory concerns around facial recognition technologies due to their inability to accurately analyze the faces of people of color and women. As can be deciphered, these are concerns not to be taken lightly. Therefore, unless facial recognition technological giants can find a way to eliminate these concerns, it is difficult to imagine a future where facial recognition technologies play a major role in our daily lives. In addition to addressing issues with the software, companies need to restore the public's trust in this software because without this, it is unlikely that people will embrace facial recognition technologies. While the benefits of facial recognition technologies are hard to ignore, privacy concerns and perceived bias in these software must be eliminated before facial recognition technologies are used on a global scale.

References

Almeida, D., Shmarko, K., & Lomas, E. (2022). The ethics of facial recognition technologies, surveillance, and accountability in an age of artificial intelligence: A comparative analysis of US, EU, and UK regulatory frameworks. AI and Ethics, 2(3), 377–387. https://doi.org/10.1007/s43681-021-00077-w

An update on our use of face recognition. (2021, November 2). Meta. https://about.fb.com/news/2021/11/update-on-use-of-face-recognition/

Facial recognition is already here: These are the 30+ us companies testing the technology. (2019, June 5). CB Insights Research. https://www.cbinsights.com/research/facial-recognition-technology-us-corporations/

Gargaro, D. (2022, December 13). The pros and cons of facial recognition technology. IT PRO. https://www.itpro.com/security/privacy/356882/the-pros-and-cons-of-facial-recognition-technology

Granitz, P. (2022, February 15). Texas sues Meta, saying it misused facial recognition data. NPR. https://www.npr.org/2022/02/15/1080769555/texas-sues-meta-for-misusing-facial-recognition-data

Heilweil, R. (2021, November 3). Facebook is backing away from facial recognition. Meta isn't. Vox. https://www.vox.com/recode/22761598/facebook-facial-recognition-meta

Klar, R. (2020, January 23). Twitter tells facial-recognition app maker to stop collecting its data. The Hill. https://thehill.com/policy/technology/479642-twitter-tells-facial-recognition-app-maker-to-stop-collecting-faces/

Kosinski, M. (2021). Facial recognition technology can expose political orientation from naturalistic facial images. Scientific Reports, 11(1), 100. https://doi.org/10.1038/s41598-020-79310-1

Liu, T., Yang, B., Geng, Y., & Du, S. (2021). Research on face recognition and privacy in china—Based on social cognition and cultural psychology. Frontiers in Psychology, 12. https://www.frontiersin.org/articles/10.3389/fpsyg.2021.809736

Lunter, J. (2020). Beating the bias in facial recognition technology. Biometric Technology Today, 2020(9), 5–7. https://doi.org/10.1016/S0969-4765(20)30122-3

Qiang, J., Wu, D., Du, H., Zhu, H., Chen, S., & Pan, H. (2022). Review on facial-recognition-based applications in disease diagnosis. Bioengineering, 9(7), 273. https://doi.org/10.3390/bioengineering9070273

Sato, M. (2022, December 5). Meta is expanding its use of AI face scanning to verify users' age on Facebook Dating. The Verge. https://www.theverge.com/2022/12/5/23494175/facebook-dating-ai-face-scanning-age-verification-expansion-yoti

Sullivan, E. (2021, September). FACIAL RECOGNITION TECHNOLOGY. Montana State Legislature . https://leg.mt.gov/content/Committees/Interim/2021-2022/Economic%20Affairs/Meetings/September%202021/facial-recognition-technology.pdf

Vincent, J. (2018, July 26). The tech industry doesn't have a plan for dealing with bias in facial recognition. The Verge. https://www.theverge.com/2018/7/26/17616290/facial-recognition-ai-bias-benchmark-test

Yoti. (2022). Yoti Age Estimation. https://www.yoti.com/wp-content/uploads/Yoti-Age-Estimation-White-Paper-May-2022.pdf

Zhang , S., Feng , Y., & Sadeh, N. (n.d.). Facial recognition: Understanding privacy concerns and attitudes across increasingly diverse deployment scenarios | usenix. Retrieved 30 December 2022, from https://www.usenix.org/conference/soups2021/presentation/zhang-shikun

SMARTPHONE BIOMETRICS

By Sapna Rameshwarsingh

Introduction

Have you ever scanned your fingerprint to unlock your phone? Or maybe unlocked your phone using face recognition? These two methods of unlocking a smartphone utilize the security mechanisms of what is known as biometrics. This term refers to the unique physiological and behavioural traits all individuals possess that can be used for identification or verification purposes. Physiological traits include facial features, fingerprints, retina scans, and iris scans whereas behavioural traits involve keystroke dynamics, handwaving, voiceprints, touchscreen dynamics, gait and other behavioural profiles to identify a user (Alzubaidi & Kalita, 2016). In this realm of technology, you may have also heard of the term 'biometric authentication'. This refers to the specific technology that uses biometric traits to identify a person or verify their identity (Gofman & Mitra, 2017). Biometric authentication has been significantly developed and widely integrated into everyday technologies over the past few years. Smartphones are a prime example of the multifaceted usage of biometrics in various applications. For example, face recognition is used to unlock phones, unlock private notes, approve downloads, and open applications such as online banking apps, e-wallets and more. Biometric authentication is so well integrated into our daily lives that we often do not realize when we are using it or how frequently we use it. As we move towards a progressively digitized world, the ability to recognize and authenticate individuals is vital to maintaining the data security of digital and non-digital information. Biometrics is an exceptional technology that evades the common threats to data security. For this reason and many others, biometrics is the most commonly used cybersecurity technology for smartphone devices as it provides cutting-edge security.

This chapter will discuss the background of biometrics in relation to smartphones, the different types of biometric data that are currently being used today, the problem of data security and the role of biometrics as a promising solution, and lastly, the lessons learned and future directions of this technology.

Biometrics: What Is It and How Does It Work?

Biometric data is categorized as either static or dynamic information. Static biometrics analyze the physiological traits of individuals such as the face, eyes, fingerprints, and hand geometry. On the other hand, dynamic biometrics examine the behavioural traits of an individual such as keypad dynamics and voice characteristics (Gofman & Mitra, 2017). Biometrics is used to identify users and verify identities, however, how exactly is this technology able to achieve this? A biometric system has three stages known as enrollment, matching, and decision (Gofman & Mitra, 2017). These three components work in tandem with one another to achieve the goals of the biometric system. In the enrollment stage, a biometric sample such as a fingerprint is collected and converted into a biometric image. This image is captured by a device commonly called the sensor. The image is then processed for feature extraction, meaning that the features being used to detect a person's identity are extracted from the image and enrolled into the system (Gofman & Mitra, 2017). In the matching stage, the enrolled image is matched against a database of features that were previously extracted from prior images. These images are commonly referred to as reference feature vectors as they provide a log of the person's features the system can use to provide correct identification. The last stage known as the decision stage, is arguably the most important stage as this provides a decision on whether the person is genuine or an imposter (Gofman & Mitra, 2017). However, it is important to note that without any of the prior stages, the decision stage would not be possible nor be able to provide accurate information.

It is also important to consider that akin to any system, this biometric system also has some limitations. Due to this three-component framework, there is scope for error with two types of error emerging at the forefront of this problem. The first source of error is known as a false acceptance rate (FAR) which occurs when an imposter is judged to be genuine by the biometric system. In other words, this error occurs when someone else is identified as the owner of the phone because the system found a match when it should not have. The second error is described as a false rejection rate (FRR) and occurs when a genuine person is judged to be an imposter. To illustrate, this error emerges when one attempts to unlock their phone however, the biometric data is not recognized. In this scenario, the system does not find a match when it in fact should have (Gofman & Mitra, 2017). FARs and FRRs are definitional characteristics of every biometric system that occur during the matching stage. This means that every system will contain some level of FAR and FRR errors. As a result of this, a predetermined threshold of FAR and FRR errors is calculated and embedded within each system. The most commonly used measure to evaluate the performance of a biometric system is called the equal error rate (ERR). This rate calculates the value where the FAR and FRR approximately coincide with each other (Gofman & Mitra, 2017).

Types of Biometric Data

Face Recognition

Now that there is a general understanding of how biometric authentication works, we can discuss in further detail the various types of biometric data that are commonly used in smartphone applications. The first type of biometric data that will be highlighted is possibly one of the most successful applications of this cybersecurity technology and is known as face recognition. Due to its versatility and effectiveness, facial detection has received a significant amount of attention over the past few years (Gofman & Mitra, 2017). It has the ability to not only identify and verify individuals from still and video images, but also from two-dimensional (2D) and three-dimensional (3D) images. This biometric system requires three steps in order to provide accurate facial recognition: detection of faces, feature extraction, and identification and/or verification. Unlike other systems, the steps involved in this biometric process can overlap and occur simultaneously with each other. For instance, face detection and feature extraction can occur simultaneously by using features such as the eyes, nose etc. to achieve their tasks (Gofman & Mitra, 2017).

Furthermore, the methods used in facial recognition have been summarized and classified into three categories which include holistic, feature-based, and hybrid methods (Gofman & Mitra, 2017). Holistic methods use the entire face as the raw input for the facial recognition system. Systems such as Eigenfaces, Fisherfaces, support vector machines, and independent component analysis all use holistic methods in their facial recognition programming. The second classification, known as feature-based methods, uses local features such as the nose, eyes, and mouth as the raw input into the recognition system. Information such as the location and local statistics (i.e. the geometric features and appearance) of these local features is detected and extracted. This input is then sent to a structural classifier which executes the recognition process. Some systems that use this type of methodology are the hidden Markov model, pure geometry methods, and graph matching methods (Gofman & Mitra, 2017). The last method which describes a hybrid approach uses both local features and the whole face region to identify faces. Techniques such as modular Eigenfaces, local feature analysis, and component-based methods all use this approach when conducting facial recognition tasks (Gofman & Mitra, 2017).

Fingerprint Scanning

Fingerprinting is one of the oldest forms of biometric data used in history. According to the Federal Bureau of Investigation (FBI), the odds of two individuals sharing the same fingerprint is one in 64 billion, making this methodology an effective solution to data security (Gofman & Mitra, 2017). Fingerprints are defined by a unique combination of global features such as valleys and ridges as well as local features like ridge endings and ridge bifurcations called minutiae. Currently, there are several fingerprint-matching techniques such as graph-based matching and genetic algorithms, however, minutiae-based fingerprint matching is the most dominant technology used in the field (Gofman & Mitra, 2017). The process of minutiae matching involves a series of steps with the first one being the extraction of minutiae features. This occurs by first conducting an orientation computation, image segmentation and image enhancement which then makes it possible to extract ridge features and minutiae from the fingerprint. It is important to note that within the scope of minutiae-based techniques, there are several substream methodologies that are used for identification and verification tasks. For example, there is the delay triangulation method, the application of correlation filters, and the distortion-tolerant filter for elastic distorted fingerprint matching (Gofman & Mitra, 2017). Nonetheless, although this type of biometric data is highly useful, it also has its limitations. Fingerprinting may provide inaccurate results if the input images are of low quality, degraded due to cuts or other natural elements, contain noise, or if there are problems with the fingerprint readers themselves (Gofman & Mitra, 2017).

Gait-Based Authentication

Gait-based biometrics is a newly developed field that uses behavioural data on an individual's gait characteristics to authenticate the user. Gait-based authentication identifies and verifies a user by analyzing the individual's walking styles such as their normal and fast walking pace (Alzubaidi & Kalita, 2016). A well-known gait-based authentication method is known as the Wearable Sensor (WS) based approach. Wearable Sensors are devices that are worn on the body of users like on the waist, belt, pockets and hands, and are used to collect various information on the individual. These sensors can include accelerometers, speed sensors, gyroscopes, and force sensors and they are able to collect behavioural information by using a motion recording system (Alzubaidi & Kalita, 2016). Gait features can be extracted using two approaches called cyclic and non-cyclic methods (Hestbek et al., 2012). Cyclic methods collect information on the gait cycles of a user and encode this data in terms of time series. The unique features identified within these cycles are then extracted and computed to create a template that is able to identify the correct user. On the other hand, non-cyclic methods function without the use of previously identified gait cycles. This technique computes the user's features by selecting time intervals during walking to capture the locations of the sensors themselves (Hestbek et al., 2012). Gait biometrics has a distinctive advantage over fingerprinting in that it is a non-intrusive technique that does not demand any cooperation from the user (Chellappa et al., 2009). In other words, this form of biometric technology provides the user with an uninterrupted experience and is able to operate at a moderate distance from the user.

Iris Recognition

Iris recognition is a type of physiological biometric data that is collected for user recognition and authentication. This type of biometric data is widely used in security applications since it involves distinctive features that rarely change over time (Minaee et al., 2016). There are many algorithms that can be used for iris recognition such as the 2D Gabor wavelet transform, a combination of features using Haar wavelet, and elastic graph matching paired with Gabor wavelet (Minaee et al., 2016). During an iris recognition task, the iris region is first segmented and then mapped onto a rectangular region in polar coordinates. After the segmented features are mapped, they are extracted and sent for further processing (Minaee et al., 2016). However, automated iris recognition also has its challenges. One of the main challenges of this technique is acquiring a high-quality image of the user's iris while utilizing non-invasive methods (Gofman & Mitra, 2017). In order for this method to be effective, images must be captured with sufficient resolution and sharpness which demands the use of advanced technology that may be costly. Current commercial iris recognition systems use digital cameras to capture high-quality images and infrared light to illuminate the iris without harming the individual. However, these devices often require more time to capture iris images compared to the time needed to capture faces and/or fingerprint images (Gofman & Mitra, 2017). Despite these challenges, this method has several advantages over other forms of biometric data. For example, similar to gait-based authentication, iris recognition uses a non-invasive method for capturing images. It also does not require the user to make physical contact with a sensor device as seen in fingerprint scanning nor perform specific actions as required for gait-based authentication and voice recognition (Gofman & Mitra, 2017).

Although only face recognition, fingerprint scanning, gait-based authentication, and iris recognition have been discussed in this section, it is important to note that there are many more types of biometric data used for cybersecurity purposes. Smartphones can use a wide range of data to verify their users which can extend from handwaving and keystroke-based authentication, to touchscreen-based authentication and voice recognition (Alzubaidi & Kalita, 2016).

Problems of Data Security

Over the years, data security has significantly evolved from old-school techniques to cutting-edge technology such as biometrics. However, several problems continue to persist in the realm of data security. These problems are highly relevant, especially in the modern world where many people have become reliant on smartphones for various personal, work-related, and other communication tasks. Due to the compact nature of smartphones, they are highly convenient for everyday use however, it also means they are prone to being lost, stolen, or accessed by non-owners (Alzubaidi & Kalita, 2016). Since many individuals tend to store their passwords and private information on their devices, data hacking threats have increased over the years (Alzubaidi & Kalita, 2016). If an intruder gains access to a smartphone device, they may have the power to impersonate the original owner and acquire monetary gains from the owner's accounts. According to statistics, the total number of lost or stolen devices in the United States increased from 1.6 million in 2012 to 3.1 million in 2013. This is a significant problem as intruders are most likely to access Online Social Networks (OSNs) and financial applications on stolen devices (Alzubaidi & Kalita, 2016). Moreover, according to a survey conducted by Breitinger and Nickel (2010), only 13% of smartphone owners use PINs or other passcodes to secure their devices. This means that approximately 87% of the surveyed individuals did not use password protection and were at risk of experiencing data hacks if their devices were lost or stolen. 74% of the individuals who did not use passwords justified their choice by stating they either wanted quick access to their data or simply because they did not think about data security. Thus, finding effective, accessible, and easy solutions to secure personal data is imperative.

Passwords and PINs are one of the most popular forms of data security that have been used for decades. They provide fast and easy encryption to secure accounts, data, and other personal information. Despite these advantages, passwords and PINs are highly susceptible to theft and guessing attempts (Gofman & Mitra, 2017). Weak passwords are susceptible to dictionary attacks wherein the intruder can compile a list of commonly used passwords and try all guesses until the correct one is found. Most dictionaries are relatively small, consisting of approximately 100,000 terms which make it easy for computers to try all passwords in just under a few minutes (Gofman & Mitra, 2017). Due to this, the prime limitation of passwords and PINs is that they are easily hacked or stolen. To further illustrate this, a study conducted on Apple users showed that the top 10 iPad passcodes were 1234, 0000, 2580, 1111, 5555, 5683, 0852, 2222, 1212, and 1998. Other common passcodes used were birth years or graduation years. The problem with using simple passcodes such as these is that they can be guessed in less than 10 attempts (Gofman & Mitra, 2017).

Another common data security technology is known as magnetic cards which have been developed since the late 1960s (Gofman & Mitra, 2017). These cards consist of multiple magnetic strips that store encoded information. However, similar to passcodes and PINs, magnetic cards can also be stolen, easily lost, forged, or duplicated (Alzubaidi & Kalita, 2016). To counteract this, smart card technology was developed to provide effective solutions for most of the limitations that accompany magnetic cards such as card duplication. These smart cards can be regarded as a credit card-sized, portable computer without a display screen or keyboard (Thales Group, 2022). It contains a microprocessor, memory, and some apps which can be used with contact or contactless card readers like ATM machines or smartphones. These cards provide an improved method to securely store data, protect communications with encryption, and identify and authenticate cardholders or other authorized individuals (Thales Group, 2022). Due to the enhanced security of these cards, they are more resistant to duplication attempts compared to magnetic cards. However, this security system can still be hacked. For example, secret codes stored in these smart cards can be extracted by using other technology to eavesdrop on the communication between the card and the card reader (Gofman & Mitra, 2017). Lastly, similar to passcodes and PINs, smart cards are also susceptible to loss and theft.

Fortunately, biometric technology is resistant to these aforementioned threats, thereby making it one of the most effective solutions for data security. Biometric security utilizes the unique biological traits of individuals which cannot be lost, stolen, duplicated, or forged (Gofman & Mitra, 2017). In addition, biometric data can be used to reduce fraud, improve the convenience of security measures as users are not required to remember long and complicated passwords, and provide a stronger security system (Prabhakar & Bjorn, 2007). For these reasons, smartphone biometric security does not face the same limitations as traditional security measures. To further illustrate, passcodes are threatened by the use of weak and easy words or numbers such as birth years, the names of family members, or a pet's name. Since biometrics does not require external data inputs, it does not face the same challenges as passcodes and PINs. Most importantly, biometrics is one of the only forms of personal security that can guarantee the authentication of a user (Prabhakar & Bjorn, 2007). For instance, passwords and tokens can be shared, stolen, or duplicated which allows intruders to use these passcodes to gain access to personal information. The security system will never be able to recognize if the person gaining access to the stored data is the authentic owner or an intruder. On the other hand, biometric security will be able to detect and distinguish between an authentic owner and an intruder which solves many of the problems associated with data security.

Future Directions of Biometrics

Over the past few decades, the world has witnessed a significant revolution in the field of communications technology. A major player in this field has been the introduction of smartphone devices which have been accompanied by cutting-edge security technology. As it currently stands in today's society, smartphones are synonymous with a necessity of life. Due to its accessibility, simplicity, and essentially infinite capability, smartphones are integrated into the daily lives of people. It is used to store personal, financial, and professional information which is why it is paramount to develop highly private and secure systems to protect this data.

The use of behavioural and physiological authentication systems such as biometrics is a promising solution to data security. It is postulated that the field of biometrics will enhance the security and usability of smartphones (Alzubaidi & Kalita, 2016). When looking at the future direction of biometrics, it is seen that although there are several methods used to evaluate the behavioural and/or physiological data, a standardized goal-standard method needs to be developed. This would ensure that there is a widely accepted metric in the field that can be used to compare the effectiveness of different approaches (Alzubaidi & Kalita, 2016). Secondly, the use of machine learning in biometrics should be further implemented as this form of artificial intelligence is well-suited to generalize and learn from prior user encounters in order to predict future authentication. Additionally, many studies using this technology operate on the assumption that a user's behaviour is consistent. However, in some situations, a user's actions may change due to personal injury or the nature of the situation like during a panicked experience. In this case, biometric security systems must still be equipped to correctly identify a user and correctly distinguish between an owner and an intruder (Alzubaidi & Kalita, 2016). With the constant and fast-paced use of smartphone devices, there is a demand for continuous authentication systems that will allow individuals to use their devices without having to frequently enter PINs and passcodes. Biometrics can provide a propitious solution to achieving continuous authentication which will make the smartphone-user experience a much easier, secure, and accessible one.

References

Alzubaidi, A., & Kalita, J. (2016). Authentication of smartphone users using behavioral biometrics. IEEE Communications Surveys & Tutorials, 18(3), 1998–2026. https://doi.org/10.1109/comst.2016.2537748

Breitinger, F., & Nickel, C. (2010). User survey on phone security and usage. In Brömme Arslan & C. Busch (Eds.), BIOSIG 2010: Biometrics and electronic signatures ; Proceedings of the Special Interest Group on biometrics and electronic signatures ; 09. - 10. September 2010 in Darmstadt, Germany (pp. 139–144). Gesellschaft für Informatik e.V.

Gofman, M., & Mitra, S. (Eds.). (2017). Biometrics in a data driven world: Trends, Technologies, and challenges. CRC PRESS.

Hestbek, M. H., Nickel, C., & Busch, C. (2012). Biometric gait recognition for mobile devices using wavelet transform and support vector machines. In 2012 19th International Conference on systems, signals and Image Processing (IWSSIP): Took place 11-13 April 2012 in Vienna, Austria (Vol. 11, pp. 57–66). IEEE.

Minaee, S., Abdolrashidiy, A., & Wang, Y. (2016). An experimental study of deep convolutional features for iris recognition. In 2013 IEEE Signal Processing in Medicine and Biology Symposium (SPMB): Polytechnic Institute of New York University, Brooklyn, NY, December 7, 2013 (pp. 1–6). IEEE.

Prabhakar, S., & Bjorn, V. (2007). Biometrics in the commercial sector. In Handbook of biometrics (pp. 479–507). essay, Scholars Portal.

Ramanathan , N., Veeraraghavan , A., & Chellappa, R. (2009). Gait Biometrics, Overview. In A. K. Jain & S. Z. Li (Eds.), Encyclopedia of biometrics (pp. 628–633). Springer.

Smart cards – an illustrated guide (2022). Thales Group. (n.d.). Retrieved December 28, 2022, from https://www.thalesgroup.com/en/markets/digital-identity-and-security/technology/smart-cards-basics#:~:text=Smart%20cards%20provide%20ways%20to,and%20protect%20communications%20with%20encryption

AIRPORT BIOMETRIC SCREENING

By Mya George

Introduction

Aviation is a critical aspect of transportation that connects individuals across individual countries and the world. It is also a critical component of local and national economies with the sector accounting for 3.6% of the global GDP, meaning that if you considered aviation as a country it would be the 20th largest by GDP (If Aviation Was A Country It Would Be The World's 20th Largest By GDP, n.d.). In an emerging post-COVID world, there has already been a large increase in the number of individuals travelling that is only expected to increase over time. These changes bring with it increasing needs for changes to the security and boarding process to be more efficient while not sacrificing functioning necessary for passenger safety and security. In this chapter, we will explore some history regarding travel, aviation and changes made since the 9/11 attacks, and the possibilities involved in incorporating biometric data collection and use in airports.

The State of Aerial Travel Before 9/11

When were passports created and how have travel permissions changed over time?

What is the current role of passports for security in international travel?

Most nation-states issue and require the possession of a valid passport to allow for legal travel and crossing of borders, but the modern day passport is a complex document that has roots before the common era (O'Byrne, 2001). The Old Testament of the Bible details an exchange between King Artaxerxes of Persia and Nehemiah, the Jewish leader who hailed from Babylon, in which Nehemiah asked for permission to travel to Judah.

Modern passports, issued by approximately 170 countries, have a variety of designs, colours. Passports are usually comprised of a hard cover that is embossed with a country's coat of arms, with pages stitched inside including personal identifiers (including an image of the individual), space for cachet stamps and visas, and also a serialized passport number. Most passports have additional security features to prevent alterations, forgery, and the production of counterfeit passports (O'Byrne, 2001). For Canadian passports, since July 1st, 2013, all passports have had an electronic component—an embedded chip (Features of the Passport - Canada.Ca, n.d.). The passport photo is both digitally printed and embedded onto the appropriate page of the passport and on the electronic chip. Holographic images on the pages of the Canadian passport are embossed in a thin-film laminate that serves to secure the personal information onto the page, to prevent it from being easily copied, and provides a unique look to the passport as the booklet reflects light differently from the normal page. Additionally, the short form term "CAN" is visible when looking through pages in a Canadian passport and there is a machine readable zone at the bottom of the pages which also contains the individual's personal and passport specific information in a specific format.

Because of the inherent value of passports and the information that they contain, the Government of Canada recommends several steps to protect oneself from passport and travel document fraud. The primary recommendation is to only use the Canadian Government's passport forms available from Canada.ca as they are the official sites, free for use, and because third party sites may be out of date (Protect Yourself from Passport and Travel Document Fraud - Canada.Ca, n.d.). Limiting who you provide scanned copies of your passport too is also important to ensure that no one uses your information for unintended purposes. In the event that your passport is compromised, you can apply to replace the travel document and can contact the passport program specifically if there are concerns of identity theft.

The Impacts of the 9/11 Attacks on Airport Security

The Events of 9/11

On September 11th, 2001, a series of terrorist attacks were carried out in New York City, the capital of the United States, Washington, D.C., and Shanksville, ending the lives of almost 3,000 people (Two Decades Later, the Enduring Legacy of 9/11 | Pew Research Center, n.d.). These attacks, where airplanes were hijacked and intentionally crashed in a way to cause mass destruction and death, were committed by militants associated with al Qaeda and Osama bid Laden, the extremist leader who founded and led al Qaeda, who later admitted to orchestrating the attacks (September 11 Attacks | History, Summary, Location, Timeline, Casualties, & Facts | Britannica, n.d.). On the morning of the attacks, groups of attackers boarded 4 different planes that were to depart three different east coast airports. Once airborne, the attackers seized control of the aircrafts by overtaking the crew onboard (some of which were reportedly stabbed). The greatest death toll was seen in the attacks against New York City, where the first plane crashed into the North Tower of the World Trade Center at 8:46am. At the time, the World Trade Center was comprised of two twin towers that boasted 110 floors home to business and governmental agencies involved in international trading (World Trade Center | History, Height, Memorial, & Facts | Britannica, n.d.). The second plane to make contact hit the other tower 17 minutes after the first, establishing that this was indeed, no accident but instead an orchestrated attack on the United States. In the emergency response effort in New York, over 400 police officers and firefighters lost their lives after rushing into the towers to save individuals working there.

The third plane struck the side of the Pentagon, the headquarters of the United States Department of Defense in Washington, D.C., at 9:37 am (September 11 Attacks | History, Summary, Location, Timeline, Casualties, & Facts | Britannica, n.d.). The final hijacked plane, with some passengers onboard informed about the attacks via their cell phones, ended up crashing in Shanksville, Pennsylvania after those onboard attempted to take back the plane from the attackers. While all passenger and crew members from that final flight were killed in the crash, their actions saved many lives as the attackers were believed to have reprogramed the flight towards the U.S. Capitol Building, where the country's legislators were in session (Flight 93 Story - Flight 93 National Memorial (U.S. National Park Service), n.d.).

How has airport security changed because of 9/11?

While this chapter will not investigate the actions taken by the United States in response to the attacks and their military efforts overall, we will explore the extent to which the 9/11 terrorist attacks changed airport security and the travel industry in whole. The 9/11 attacks were highly impactful, for the scale and source of the attacks, the number of lives that were taken, and even in terms of visuals where a notable piece of the New York City skyline was destroyed–at the center of the largest city in the United States. What was experienced by the U.S. realistically could have impacted any other developed nation and so immediate change to the way in which people traversed the globe became a primary concern of governments.

In direct response to the 9/11 attacks, the United States government brought forth new legislation to protect passenger's safety and security. The first of this was the Aviation and Transportation Security Act signed into law by the then President, George W. Bush, which mandated additions to security procedures and tasked the Department of Transportation with implementing them, under the creation of the Transportation Security Administration (TSA) (Blalock et al., 2007). Due to increased security measures after 9/11, airlines began suggesting that passengers arrive at the airport at least 2 hours before their domestic flight was scheduled to take-off. Random selection was implemented in the passenger screening process to subject some individuals to additional screening, potentially including searching through their bags by hand, full body scanning, and/or a partial or full body pat down. In the initial changes carried out by the TSA, a larger number of staff were hired to carry out greater screening and security needs, individuals involved in airport screening were compensated with higher wages and increased benefits, and greater training was provided to staff (Blalock et al., 2007). Previous to the 9/11 attacks, there was no established system for reviewing the contents of passenger's bags and only 5% of baggage was ever searched (THE 9/11 COMMISSION REPORT, n.d.). The TSA created two rounds of deadlines for airports to meet certain criteria for changes to baggage review, where under the first deadline airlines either had to implement positive bag matching where each bag was connected to a passenger onboard a select flight (ensuring that no baggage is boarded if the passenger does not board themselves as might be a tactic employed by individuals attempting to illicit harm without themselves being harmed) or checked baggage needed to undergo explosives screening using an approved method (49 U.S. Code § 44901 - Screening Passengers and Property | U.S. Code | US Law | LII / Legal Information Institute, n.d.; Blalock et al., 2007). By January 2003, 90% of checked baggage in the United States were benign screened electronically (Blalock et al., 2007).

The case in Canada

Previous to the events of 9/11, an Air India flight that was travelling from Montreal to London to Delhi and then to Mumbai (which was named Bombay at the time) on June 23rd, 1985, when, before reaching London, a planted bomb on the plane resulted in its disintegration close to the Irish coast (Air India Flight 182 Disaster | Cause, Investigation, & Ireland | Britannica, n.d.). The flight had originally departed from Toronto before stopping in Montreal, where Canadian personnel removed three suspicious looking packages from the plane. While the aircraft was 45 minutes out from Heathrow Airport in London, it blew up without any warning and while emergency crews were dispatched, no survivors were found and less than half of the passenger's bodies were able to be recovered (Air India Flight 182 Disaster | Cause, Investigation, & Ireland | Britannica, n.d.). While the source of the disaster was not immediately known, two suspects were arrested five months later with one of them later pleading guilty to manslaughter connected to the event in 2003 and was sentenced to 5 years in prison (Air India Flight 182 Disaster | Cause, Investigation, & Ireland | Britannica, n.d.). While others were arrested in connection to the disaster, they were released due to insufficient evidence. The Canadian investigation found that a group of radical Sikh Canadians were most likely behind the attack with a bomb having been manufactured and flown in a suitcase from Vancouver to Toronto where it was put on the flight departing for London, England (Lessons to Be Learned, n.d.). Because this flight took place in the summertime, those on board were largely Canadian families with children travelling to visit relatives and young tourists who all perished alongside the aircraft's crew.

Under procedures established by the airline, Air India, all baggage for the flight had been subjected to additional security checks–which was more than any other Canadian or international airline at the time (Lessons to Be Learned, n.d.). However, at the time it was possible to check baggage without boarding the aircraft as the baggage could still be authorized under the ticket that had been purchased. Information provided from Transport Canada reported that checked baggage was not physically checked for this flight, nor was a headcount done prior to departure (Air India Flight 182 Disaster | Cause, Investigation, & Ireland | Britannica, n.d.). There was an x-ray unit that was new to the Toronto airport security that was used to review baggage but it became unserviceable before everything could go through security, and no baggage was physically examined (Lessons to Be Learned, n.d.). Many mistakes were made along the process allowing a homemade bomb to be flown from Vancouver to Toronto, costing 329 lives. Since this disaster in 1985, the Canadian Department of Foreign Affairs has organized 24 hour operations in Ottawa that continuously respond to disaster events and coordinate relief efforts and necessary supports (Lessons to Be Learned, n.d.).

The Implementation of Biometric-Based Screening in Airports

What are biometrics?

Biometrics refer to specific measurements, calculations, and analysis that detail specifics of an individual's physical and be-

havioural traits. Soft biometrics in particular refer to characteristics that offer insight into one's physical and behavioural
traits without a level of detail that can allow one to differen-
tiate between any two individuals (Ricanek & Barbour, 2011).
This classification includes specific measures to evaluate facial
features, as the size and shape of the lips, chin, nose, eye-
brows, and other features which can be used to determine
biological sex, race and ethnicity, and (with the aid of lines,
creases, and wrinkles in the skin) can estimate age (Ricanek &
Barbour, 2011). While most research on soft biomarkers has
centered on the face, further efforts have and continue to investigate characteristics such as one's gait, hand, the iris of the
eye, and the area around the eye to gain better insights from
biometric observations.

How are biometrics currently being used?

An important consideration in the implementation of biometric data collection and review for travel purposes, at least relating to the review of digital photos, is based on a process
that has been used for a considerable time in aviation–when
an aviation worker checks one's photo ID and compares it to
the person in front of them. The transition to relying on ma-
chine-based collection of biometric data and their analysis
is currently being tested and implemented in select circumstances to better improve accuracy in identifying individuals
and enhancing airport security.

In Canada, the Government has set biometric collection to include all temporary resident visa, work permit, study permit,
and temporary resident permit applicants who are not residents of the United States of America (Biometrics Screening,
n.d.). Since July of 2018, applicants from Europe, Africa, and the
Middle East have been subject to biometric collection, while
applicants from Asia, the Asian Pacific, and the Americas have
had to do the same since December of the same year. However, this collection of fingerprints and digital headshots are

not required for children under the age of 14, adults over the age of 79, nor diplomats travelling for state business (Biometrics Screening, n.d.). At major airports in the country Primary Inspection Kiosks have been set up to verify the identities of travellers, where fingerprints are compared to those collected at the time of their application to ensure that the traveller is the same person who has been granted a visa or permit to enter Canada. Currently, Canadian citizens and those who have applied for Canadian citizenship are exempt from having biometrical data collected at Canadian airports.

As of August 2022, several hundred check-in and boarding kiosks from the Swiss Aviation IT company SITA were deployed across three Canadian airports: Pearson International in Toronto, Calgary International, and Montreal-Trudeau International (Three Canadian Airports Getting Biometrics-Ready Kiosks from SITA | Biometric Update, n.d.). While not all of these machines are equipped to collect biometric data, some have that as a key function and are expected to play a role in speeding up passenger screening. While there has been limited information published regarding the use of SITA's technology in Canada's biometric screening, the company has received recent investment to continue the development of their aviation-related technology, including biometric systems (Three Canadian Airports Getting Biometrics-Ready Kiosks from SITA | Biometric Update, n.d.).

In the United States, the TSA has been testing and evaluating the use of biometric technology for security, operational efficiency, and to have a more streamlined process for American travellers (Pons & Polak, 2008). These efforts include facial matching testing where a photo taken of a passenger is directly compared to the image on their ID using Credential Authentication Technology 2 (CAT-2). This does not require any upload of a photo ID in advance as it will compare the likeness of the individual and their ID at their time of travel. Participation in biometric identity recognition is currently done on a volunteer basis with the TSA, and passengers are able to choose to go through the common ID verification process instead. While preliminary work in biometric identity confirmation has and will continue to focus on passengers, future efforts are expected to include various aviation workers and law enforcement officers for additional safety and security. Furthermore, in line with the Department of Homeland Security's Fair Information Practice Principles, the TSA only retains personal and identifiable information for the necessary amount of time to achieve a conclusion from the intended testing purpose related to a particular biometric technology pilot (The Fair Information Practice Principles | Homeland Security, n.d.). There are also additional measures in place such as limitations on the use of data and data minimisation for protection purposes.

The biggest difference in the approach of integrating biometrics into airport security between Canada and the US is the intended purpose at this moment in time. While Canada's efforts have largely focussed on being able to better identify and verify the identity of foreigners, the United States has used their trial of biometric data collection to work towards meeting expectations set out in President Joe Biden's Executive Order on Transforming Customer experience, to make identity confirmation a more streamlined process in airports and to reduce points of contact between individuals (especially in light of the COVID-19 pandemic and the ways in which the travel and transportation industry has been changed by the ongoing pandemic) in addition to providing more accurate and reliable methods for identity verification (Executive Order on Transforming Federal Customer Experience and Service Delivery to Rebuild Trust in Government | The White House, n.d.; The Fair Information Practice Principles | Homeland Security, n.d.). In this Executive Order, Biden expresses the desire for the Federal Government and its agencies to deliver services in an accessible manner without unnecessary burden on customers nor on the administrative side (Executive Order on Transforming

Federal Customer Experience and Service Delivery to Rebuild Trust in Government | The White House, n.d.).

Since 2013, Customs and Border Protection (CBP) has primarily developed the biometric technology systems utilized across American airports. In 2016, CBP launched a collaboration with Delta Airlines where photo recognition was tested across multiple flights as part of a pilot project. Over a year of testing with different flight destinations, to better ensure that the software could perform accurately for different groups of people, the facial recognition software was deemed to perform with a high degree of accuracy. Additional efforts have since been made to integrate such facial recognition into the typical boarding process, rather than adding on another step for travellers to undergo before or after their flight.

Future Implications of Biometrics in Airports

Improved Integration of Existing Systems with Biometrics

In a system that is continuously working to improve its ability to identify passengers, review contents of baggage to ensure no dangerous items or goods make their way onto domestic and international flights, and to improve overall efficiency and the passenger experience, biometrics offer a unique opportunity to improve accuracy and efficiency. Accurate identification of passengers is essential not only to identify fraudulent documentation and attempts to enter a country under false circumstances but also to identify and prevent a variety of threats (Hilton, 2016). One of the greatest potentials of biometrics is to improve the identification of passengers by verifying one's identity through measuring biometrics such as fingerprint or iris scanning (Khan & Efthymiou, 2021). Additionally, with the increase in self-service type kiosks for checking in and some other necessary components of air travel, biometric identity verification has the potential to be integrated into such systems. Reducing the contact between individuals has been necessary in recent years due to the COVID-19 pandemic but also have some benefits that persist today such as allowing passengers to make progress in the steps necessary for them to board regardless of staffing at the time they arrive to the airport (as self-service machines will continuously be there) and it eliminates some sources of human error by relying on machines to take and process biometric data. The act of collecting biometric data is becoming more normalized with time. An example of this is that fingerprints have been commonly used in amusement parks like Disneyland and Universal Studios to verify individuals seeking re-entry into the parks (Privacy at the Walt Disney World Resort, the Disneyland Resort, and Aulani, a Disney Resort & Spa - The Walt Disney Privacy Center, n.d.).

Integrating the use of biometrics for all passengers, not just resident applicants (as in Canada) or those who opt into biometric screening (as in the U.S.), has the potential to provide quicker and more accurate identity verification compared to traditional methods relying on resemblance to one's passport or other forms of government-issued ID (Khan & Efthymiou, 2021). Additionally, with further development there is the ability to further improve such systems with the inclusion of artificial intelligence to allow for advanced detection for facial recognition and imaging (Verma et al., 2021). Ultimately, coming to consult biometrics instead of traditional ID systems allows for a greater degree of certainty surrounding one's identity–forgoing some challenges with items such as passports where one is simply visually verifying based on the printed image.

The way in which the integration of biometrics is most commonly presented is under a single token ID, where the passenger would be able to complete their check-in, bag drop, security, outbound immigration, and boarding process using facial recognition or another form of biometric data collection instead of repeatedly presenting one's passport and boarding pass ("Airport Passenger Processing Technology: A Biometric Airport Journey," 2018). This biometric token then replaces the passport as the passenger navigates the airport, and it would be more effective in ensuring that the individual is who they claim to be.

Conclusion

Since biometrics such as one's fingerprint is a permanent association with an individual (as although one's fingerprints can be changed by permanently damaged by some injuries or even some therapies given to cancer patients, the skin tissue usually regenerates and it is a less common issue) the potential for biometric data to be released is a massive concern related to their collection in the first place ("Airport Passenger Processing Technology: A Biometric Airport Journey," 2018; Harmon, n.d.). While greater research and work is necessary to bring about systems to protect the growing amount of data being held at airports at a regular basis as biometric data collection increases in its scope of practice, the potential of this technology and its ability to strengthen identity verification and consequently safety and security, it is in the writer's opinion that we continue to investigate the use of biometrics in airports.

References

49 U.S. Code § 44901 - Screening passengers and property | U.S. Code | US Law | LII / Legal Information Institute. (n.d.). Retrieved December 26, 2022, from https://www.law.cornell.edu/uscode/text/49/44901

Airport Passenger Processing Technology: A Biometric Airport Journey. (2018). Doctoral Dissertations and Master's Theses.

Air India Flight 182 disaster | Cause, Investigation, & Ireland | Britannica. (n.d.). Retrieved December 27, 2022, from https://www.britannica.com/event/Air-India-Flight-182-disaster

Biometrics screening. (n.d.). Retrieved December 29, 2022, from https://www.cbsa-asfc.gc.ca/security-securite/biometrics-biometrique-eng.html

Blalock, G., Kadiyali, V., & Simon, D. H. (2007). The impact of post 9/11 airport security measures on the demand for air travel. The Journal of Law and Economics, 50(4), 731–755. https://doi.org/10.1086/519816

Executive Order on Transforming Federal Customer Experience and Service Delivery to Rebuild Trust in Government | The White House. (n.d.). Retrieved December 29, 2022, from https://www.whitehouse.gov/briefing-room/presidential-actions/2021/12/13/executive-order-on-transforming-federal-customer-experience-and-service-delivery-to-rebuild-trust-in-government/

Features of the passport - Canada.ca. (n.d.). Retrieved December 29, 2022, from https://www.canada.ca/en/immigration-refugees-citizenship/services/canadian-passports/about/passport-features.html

Flight 93 Story - Flight 93 National Memorial (U.S. National Park Service). (n.d.). Retrieved December 26, 2022, from https://www.nps.gov/flni/learn/historyculture/flight93story.htm

Harmon, K. (n.d.). Can You Lose Your Fingerprints? - Scientific American.

Hilton, C. (2016). Fingerprints: A New Means of Identification in Airport Security Screening. 81, 561.

If Aviation Was A Country It Would Be The World's 20th Largest By GDP. (n.d.). Retrieved December 26, 2022, from https://www.forbes.com/sites/jamesasquith/2020/04/06/if-aviation-was-a-country-it-would-be-the-worlds-20th-largest-by-gdp/?sh=28a7bf62e5b5

Khan, N., & Efthymiou, M. (2021). The use of biometric technology at airports: The case of customs and border protection (CBP). International Journal of Information Management Data Insights, 1(2), 100049. https://doi.org/10.1016/j.jjimei.2021.100049

Lessons to be learned. (n.d.). Retrieved December 27, 2022, from https://www.publicsafety.gc.ca/cnt/rsrcs/pblctns/lssns-lrnd/index-en.aspx

O'Byrne, D. J. (2001). On passports and border controls. Annals of Tourism Research, 28(2), 399–416. https://doi.org/10.1016/S0160-7383(00)00050-5

Pons, A. P., & Polak, P. (2008). Understanding user perspectives on biometric technology. Communications of the ACM, 51(9), 115. https://doi.org/10.1145/1378727.1389971

Privacy at the Walt Disney World Resort, the Disneyland Resort, and Aulani, a Disney Resort & Spa - The Walt Disney Privacy Center. (n.d.). Retrieved December 26, 2022, from https://privacy.thewaltdisneycompany.com/en/resortfaqs/

Protect yourself from passport and travel document fraud
- Canada.ca. (n.d.). Retrieved December 29, 2022, from
https://www.canada.ca/en/immigration-refugees-citizen-
ship/services/canadian-passports/security/protect-fraud.
html

Ricanek, K., & Barbour, B. (2011). What are soft biometrics
and how can they be used? Computer, 44(9), 106–108.
https://doi.org/10.1109/MC.2011.296

September 11 attacks | History, Summary, Location, Timeline,
Casualties, & Facts | Britannica. (n.d.). Retrieved December
26, 2022, from https://www.britannica.com/event/Septem-
ber-11-attacks

THE 9/11 COMMISSION REPORT. (n.d.).

The Fair Information Practice Principles | Homeland Security.
(n.d.). Retrieved December 29, 2022, from https://www.
dhs.gov/publication/privacy-policy-guidance-memoran-
dum-2008-01-fair-information-practice-principles

Three Canadian airports getting biometrics-ready kiosks
from SITA | Biometric Update. (n.d.). Retrieved December
29, 2022, from https://www.biometricupdate.com/202208/
three-canadian-airports-getting-biometrics-ready-ki-
osks-from-sita

Two Decades Later, the Enduring Legacy of 9/11 | Pew Re-
search Center. (n.d.). Retrieved December 26, 2022, from
https://www.pewresearch.org/politics/2021/09/02/two-de-
cades-later-the-enduring-legacy-of-9-11/

Verma, S., Sharma, R., Deb, S., & Maitra, D. (2021). Artificial intelligence in marketing: Systematic review and future research direction. International Journal of Information Management Data Insights, 100002. https://doi.org/10.1016/j.jjimei.2020.100002

World Trade Center | History, Height, Memorial, & Facts | Britannica. (n.d.). Retrieved December 26, 2022, from https://www.britannica.com/topic/World-Trade-Center

CCTV SURVEILLANCE

By Abeer Ansari

CCTV stands for Closed-Circuit Television System and it is a system of cameras that relay signals in the form of videos and images to a set of monitors or screens (Sullivan, 2021). Based on the name, it can be inferred that these systems of cameras are like a closed, independently connected circuit. It is likely that you have come across many CCTV cameras of different kinds in different places - they are almost everywhere in this day and age - around traffic lights, buildings, banks and even for personal use at homes and other private properties. It is important to understand the history of CCTV cameras and how they have evolved to their widely spread use in the modern world (Sullivan, 2021).

The earliest CCTV surveillance technology is believed to have been in Germany dating back to 1942 (Sullivan, 2021). This first of its kind CCTV surveillance technology was engineered by Walter Bruch, who was an engineer, who set up the CCTV surveillance to monitor the launch of the world's first ballistic missiles during World War II. These CCTV cameras were used by the German military to stay on the lookout for rocket launches while hiding in a safe. The CCTV cameras allowed them to monitor these rockets from a distance. At that time, the CCTV technology was not advanced enough to record the live streaming of the surveillance, hence the Germany military at that time were only able to observe the live launches of rockets, but did not have access to the surveillance recordings (Sullivan, 2021). A few years later, 1949, CCTV surveillance systems were first seen in commercial settings, with the first one being at an American company called Vericon, which was an American company that manufactured and distributed live monitoring technology. Then later in 1953, CCTV surveillance cameras were brought in use when Queen Elizabeth II was being crowned in the United Kingdom. It can be observed how CCTV cameras gradually went from being used in highly intense settings such as the battlefield, to being commercialised, to then being used during personal and large community festivities. Soon after the crowning of Queen Elizabeth II, CCTV cameras were installed in streets across London for security and safety purposes, especially when the Royal Family members were present at community events or were out in public. The city of New York also started installing CCTV cameras at its streets across the city. Then in 1969, CCTV surveillance systems made its way into homes for personal security and safety use. Marie Van Brittan Brown and her husband invented a security surveillance system that would allow one to view a person standing outside their home door and hear people across different rooms within their homes. This couple from Queens, New York was awarded a patent for inventing a first of its kind home security system. Many current day home security systems are built on this initial invention (Sullivan, 2021).

CCTV surveillance systems also became popular in Retail stores, and today, almost every retail store - big or small - has some kind of CCTV security system in place (The Evolution of Closed-Circuit Television (CCTV) Systems, 2021). CCTV cameras in stores are usually found above cash registers as it allows them to monitor activity on sales as well as capture any activity of potential thefts. They are also installed at the entrance and other unique spots across the store that would capture a large area in order to aid in any potential investigations when it comes to identify potential suspects or missing persons. The use of CCTV cameras became common use in stores during the 1970s and 1980s. These CCTV surveillance system cameras would be monitored by initials hired to specifically monitor multiple screens at the same time that would cover a wide range of surveillance area, real-time, and these individuals were trained to be skilled at capturing any unusual activity and analysing the livestream in real time. However, with the increase in instalment of CCTV surveillance systems, potential threats and thieves became increasingly aware of them and in order to maintain the effectiveness if the surveillance systems, Camera domes were invented around 1980s with the purpose of protecting the surveillance systems and making them less obvious by concealing the view and movements of the CCTV cameras. Some stores even started installing fake or unoperational CCTV cameras in order to deter shoplifters from engaging in any illegal activities (The Evolution of Closed-Circuit Television (CCTV) Systems, 2021).

A significant development in the evolution of CCTV cameras took place when video cassette recorders (VCRs) became commonly available. The VCRs were considered a significant development because they allowed for the opportunity to leave the live recording up and running while it also gets saved in the VCR cassettes as a recording which can later be retrieved and played to replay any important instances or capture any information for personal or legal use. This also eased the responsibility on individuals who were hired to monitor and capture details from the CCTV surveillance cameras - in case they missed something or had to step away from the monitoring screens, they can easily rewind and capture the missed streaming. Lastly, in the 1990s, technology started to advance and big and small tweaks were being made to the CCTV systems. One of such developments was the availability of multiplex solutions. This allowed CCTV footage from different cameras to be viewed on one single monitor and this was a great advancement for many specific cases where such viewing provided great insight and ease in observation and capturing of information from different locations and angles. Around this time, color cameras were also becoming available, as opposed to the black and white cameras which increased quality in a drastic way (Fisher, 2021).

This was a brief history and evolution of the CCTV Cameras and how certain historical events have been tied with the development and advancements in the CCTV Surveillance technology. Now that the history has been understood and discussed, it is important to look at the pros and cons of using CCTV surveillance in today's digital world and how CCTV surveillance is viewed in regards to privacy and threat to privacy and confidentiality.

A CCTV system's principal goal is to enable you to view everything that occurs in a certain region (The Evolution of Closed-Circuit Television (CCTV) Systems, 2021). It can help parents monitor the CCTV recordings to watch how the family is doing while they are away form the kids at home due to work or personal reasons. Similarly, an officer could quickly replay the CCTV footage to help with an investigation. A surveillance system can enable you to conduct additional useful things, both at work and at home, in addition to just reducing crime. An office camera can increase productivity at a job since the manager may have access to recordings that demonstrate how efficiently employees are working. They have a precise record of the employees' daily routines thanks to the ability to monitor them. You can keep an eye on your employees' punctuality as well. You can keep track of when an employee arrives and departs thanks to a CCTV camera. With video proof, you can better understand why an employee is frequently late and how to prevent it. You can find misplaced objects at home with the use of a CCTV system. You can utilize a monitoring system to demonstrate if an item was lost by you or someone else in the house while demonstrating that someone broke in and stole it. CCTV has been proven to reduce crime in the UK by up to 50%, leading to the closure of 50% more cases than they otherwise would have. Unquestionably, CCTVs can lower crime rates in both public and private environments, including homes and workplaces. Security cameras can make some people feel very comfortable, but they can also make other parties feel uneasy. Because of the following factors, many people do not find these technologies particularly alluring. As a result, many people are frequently bothered by the sight of a camera nearby. Now this chapter will highlight some of the pros and cons of CCTV surveillance (The Evolution of Closed-Circuit Television (CCTV) Systems, 2021).

Installing home security cameras increases house safety from external threats such as burglary or even from people who may be a personal threat. Similarly, installing CCTV cameras in public places increases public safety in spaces such as shopping and travelling. Public crime rates can also be controlled through the use of CCTVs. Having such cameras installed at crossroads, retail stores, parking lots, concerts, conferences, museums, banks and many other public community spots. Due to the instalment of these surveillance cameras, many crimes are prevented before they even occur. For example, if a suspicious person is seen in multiple locations through the cameras, then authorities can be contacted and they arrive in those areas to get a hold of those individuals before they commit any crime. Due to this sense of safety, public fear of crimes is also reduced. The National Center for Education Statistics conducted a survey which highlighted that in 2015 about 80% of public schools installed surveillance systems in order to secure school grounds (The Evolution of Closed-Circuit Television (CCTV) Systems, 2021).

Statistics show that crime rates have been reduced by the installment of CCTV cameras. When an individual knows that there are cameras installed in an area then people will be less motivated to commit crimes. For example, stores such as Walmart have installed CCTV surveillance cameras to deter people from stealing. If a crime is carried out in an area where CCTV cameras were present, then the chances of catching those criminals are significantly increased. Software such as facial recognition have significantly improved over the years and therefore, if the criminal is found on the CCTV recordings then legal authorities will be able to recognize and catch them easily through facial recognition features. In the cases where the criminal is out and about, posters can be created with a hypothetical image of what the criminal may look like through the help of facial recognition and construction software installed within the CCTV cameras which then generates posters that can be put up around cities and local public spots through which the general public can keep an eye out and stay on high alert and when they do come across a person they identify as the potential criminal, they can easily contact authorities and track them down. Without CCTV cameras, identifying potential criminals and threats, especially with precision, can be extremely difficult despite having eye witnesses (Fisher, 2021).

The Help Of Cctv Surveillance Cameras During The Boston Marathon Bombing

A great real life experience of how CCTV surveillance helped authorities arrest a criminal was during the bombing at the Boston Marathon - with the assistance of CCTV surveillance images, it took the FBI as little as only 3 days to release the images of the potential bomber and with the help of this they were able to arrest him (Johnson, 2013). Video was the key critical factor in finding the bombers who were responsible for the Boston Marathon bombing. The police were starting to secure the footage right after the bombing took place before the first responders even arrived on scene. One of the qualities of CCTV surveillance cameras that were mentioned earlier in this chapter was their potential of having a network of interconnected closed circuit cameras and this network of cameras that were monitoring the entire area of Boston downtown were extremely helpful in helping the police secure the video footage of the bomber. Downtown Boston was being watched by over 147 surveillance cameras (Johnson, 2013). On the path that was set up for the marathon, most if not all businesses had surveillance cameras. On this marathon path, every ATM and traffic lights also had cameras installed. Grant Fredricks, who is a forensic video analyst and teacher who teaches forensic video techniques at the FBI National Academy in Quantico says that analyzing video and sorting through them is the new standard of handling public crimes. He mentions that video recordings hold more evidence than many other sources of evidence, even more so than DNA and eye-witness testimonies. However, given that CCTV video recordings are such important pieces of evidence, this also makes it one of the most risky ones to preserve and therefore, it is important to get a hold of them before someone erases the data. Moving forward, Grant Fredric hopes that every police department, regardless of how big or small it is, will have a system in place to analyse video evidence just like any other piece of evidence is analysed when it comes to solving crimes and treating legal pieces of evidence in court (Johnson, 2013). Going back to how vital the CCTV cameras were in the Boston attack, it was the cameras that were installed outside a department store called Lord & Taylor which were the first to capture a glimpse of two men who allegedly bombed the Boston Marathon (Johnson, 2013). Stewart Baker, the Homeland Security official who saw the events unfold at the Marathon, said that similar CCTV images that were found in the CCTV during the marathon, helped authorities track the individuals who bombed the London Subway station in 2015. Such real life cases highlight the importance of having CCTV surveillance cameras not only in legal and authorised places but also in public spaces in order to capture events that one may not be expecting (Johnson, 2013).

In today's day and age, personal privacy in both private and public spaces is extremely important. With the rise in technology advancements, breach of privacy is a real concern.

Therefore, this chapter will now discuss some of the concerns associated with CCTV surveillance cameras. Firstly, the CCTV surveillance systems can be easily abused (Li, 2022). Many of the CCTV surveillance cameras are installed in public spaces and this also increases the concern of them being abused by the people who have installed them. For example, law enforcements that monitor individuals through the CCTV surveillance cameras networks may misuse the captured information and use it as a form of blackmail (Li, 2022). Another form of CCTV surveillance abuse is voyeurism - this is the act of spying on women in public spaces and this can be extremely inappropriate in some cases. In many cases Voyeurism can be charged as a criminal offence. It is defined as a sexual preference for watching adult females especially when they are in extremely vulnerable states. The cases of such acts through the CCTV cameras usually take place in areas that are not well developed or monitored by legal authorities and include spots such as changing rooms of stores, public washrooms and other women only areas. With the advancements and increase in installations of CCTV cameras across the world, the need to put in place safety measures that ensures privacy and confidentiality has significantly increased, however, due to advancements in technologies, scamming and hackers, there is yet to have a solution which guarantees members ultimate privacy and security (Li, 2022). Another downside of installing CCTV camera networks in public spaces is how expensive it is. Many people argue that if CCTV surveillance is not 100% effective in preventing crimes then what is the point of investing so much money in installing these cameras in public spaces. For example, the officials in Michigan from the American Civil Liberties union were proposing to install a large amount of CCTV surveillance cameras across the country but then concluded with the decision of not putting them up as they were unable to justify the high cost appointed with installment and maintenance of such cameras (Li, 2022).

Now that we have discussed the history of CCTV surveillance cameras as well as their pros and cons, this chapter will now shed light on the future of CCTV surveillance systems (Whittaker, 2021). When discussing the future of CCTV surveillance, it is important to talk about AI CCTV surveillance cameras (Whittaker, 2021). AI security cameras are specialised network IP cameras that perform highly advanced functions such as detection of vehicles, face detection, person detection, counting and traffic analysis, people count analysis and licence plate recognition (LPR). These AI systems software are built-in to the CCTV surveillance systems that have been described in this chapter. In order for AI CCTV cameras to operate efficiently, the data being collected through the camera gets sent to a recorder and is then processed through an AI software which uses its analytics to make sense of the raw video that gets captured (Whittaker, 2021). AI CCTV cameras also have a sub-kind called Rule-bases AI cameras. In the rule-based AI cameras, the user can manually set-up rules and reference images of humans and other regulations - when the AI comes across any manually entered images or rules, then it makes decisions accordingly. For example, if there is a rule set in place which states "no one is allowed in this area after 8 PM" then if the CCTV camera records anyone in the area after 8 PM, then it will send an alert. Some of the AI CCTV surveillance cameras also engage in self-learning and this happens with behavioural analytic software. With this technology, when CCTV cameras are installed in a specific area, the AI system monitors the behaviours that are taking place in that area and gradually learns that this is the "normal" or "typical" behaviour. The learnt behaviour includes the speed, size, and colour of objects and people. Once the AI understands this normal pattern of behaviour, it can then spot any object or person that is deviating from this typical behaviour and can then send an alert for security purposes (Whittaker, 2021). The CCTV cameras that have been discussed earlier are helpful in solving crimes by going through the recorded footage, however, with AI CCTV cameras, the alerts can be sent to authorities in real time which makes the process of legal investigation and prevention much more efficient. One more advancement that people may see in the future of CCTV surveillance is the use of two-way audio systems. These will allow for operators to speak with anyone who is in the area where the CCTV cameras are installed. Speaking of audio systems, there will also be the possibility of having pre-recorded audio based announcements play through the surveillance cameras (Whittaker, 2021).

References

Fisher, D. (2021, January 20). The evolution of closed-circuit television (CCTV) systems. Vector Security Networks.

The history of CCTV – from 1942 to present. PCR. (2014, September 2).

Ivc. (2021, July 9). CCTV camera system: Knowing the pros and cons - the leader in Industrial Video Solutions. IVC.

Johnston, B. (2022, September 14). A brief history of surveillance cameras. Deep Sentinel.

Reolink. (n.d.). Top 8 pros and cons of surveillance cameras in public places - reolink blog. Reolink.

Whittaker, D. (2021, December 13). Why AI CCTV is the future of security and surveillance in public spaces. Security Magazine RSS.

SMART HOME TECHNOLOGY AND SECURITY

By Ryan Doleweerd

What Is A Smart Home?

A smart home is a modern home that allows a tenant to interact with it by using different types of technology that can be remotely accessed through a central computer control system or uses artificial intelligence to improve the life of the tenant (Mulcahy et al., 2019). How smart a smart home is, is dependent on the number of interactive devices and sensors within it (Harper, 2003). These different types of technology are things like smart personal assistants such as the Amazon Echo and the Google Home, security cameras like the Google Nest cam, high-tech household appliances like the Roomba vacuum and smart lights, and other home automation technology (Mulcahy et al., 2019). The goal of the smart home is to respond to the occupants' needs to better improve their comfort, security, management, and entertainment (Harper, 2003).

Smart Grid Integration

The goal of the smart grid is to enhance the infrastructure of the power grid where electricity runs through being transmitted, distributed, and consumed. It was created as a countermeasure to climate change, reducing energy cost as old infrastructure is replaced and electricity prices are going up. A smart grid enhances the power grid infrastructure by integrating measurement technologies, sensor technology, other advanced components and integrated communication technology into the existing grid. This allows for the smart grid to monitor energy flow and usage. This allows for electricity to be used efficiently as the smart grid is able to monitor and reduce the amount of energy loss that occurs. It can generate more energy at peak usage times and generate less during off times for economical benefits. This is useful in smart homes as many smart appliances have smart grid integrations that allow the appliance to minimise energy usage for reasons like reducing impact on climate change and reducing its energy cost of using the appliance (Nepveu & Diaz, 2010). As there are many sensors and control systems used within the smart grid, and its goal is to enhance the tenants life, the smart grid is an important part of smart home technology as it manages and minimises energy usage of the tenant while ensuring their power bill is not large (Harper, 2003; Nepveu & Diaz, 2010).

Smart Personal Assistants

A smart personal assistant will receive input from the user, through voice commands or from an app, and execute the task. For example, with the Google Home smart assistant, it can receive commands like "turn off the lights" and will turn off the smart lights that have been paired, or it could be told to play a song, and it will search the connected music library to play the song. A smart personal assistant is now essentially a multipurpose command centre of smart technology in a smart home in addition to a smartphone (Mulcahy et al., 2019).

A smart personal assistant is a device that has now added another method through which human computer interaction can be conducted. Typically, this interaction was done through physical methods, like a mouse and keyboard or a joystick (Edu et al., 2021). This new avenue uses voice recognition software to understand what we are saying and execute the command being asked of it. This uses artificial intelligence to understand and learn from its environment so it can maximise its success rate. A device that has artificial intelligence is one that is aware of its environment and takes action based on inputs it perceives to maximise a successful outcome. Artificial intelligence is the ability of a device to mimic human intelligence (Guo et al., 2019). Then machine learning occurs by receiving inputs from its environment and finding patterns and trends among the inputs that correlate to different outputs. With more inputs, the outcome becomes more accurate and successful. For smart personal assistants, the input is sound, and it learns as it gains experience and can better recognize and understand the user's voice (Koteluk et al., 2021). The success of these smart personal assistants is shown off by how often they are used. In a survey done in the United States, approximately 69 percent of smart assistant owners use their smart assistant every day, almost half of the homes in the United States have a smart assistant, and one-third of the homes in the United States are planning on purchasing a smart assistant in the next few years (Sweeney & Davis, 2021).

Smart Assistants and Privacy

With almost half of the houses in the United States owning a smart assistant and that number increases day by day, privacy is a large concern. As useful as these assistants are, the data infrastructures are heavily controlled by the company that designs these smart assistants like Google and Amazon. The lack of personal control over a user's smart assistant makes users uneasy about their privacy and confidentiality. They ask "Is my smart assistant listening and recording my conversations?" This is because the level of privacy and confidentiality is not clear or guaranteed by the company that designs these assistants (Sweeney & Davis, 2021). There are questions of user consent to data collection that are not explicitly asked by these smart assistants, hence the concern over personal data confidentiality and privacy. One counterargument is that ownership of the device is up to the owner, and confidentiality may not be worth it to the user if the personal benefit is greater than the possible breach of privacy. (Birchley et al., 2017). One risk is the sharing of personal health information, which might be overheard by the smart assistant, and collected, which is a scary thought for many people (Suresh & Sruthi, 2015). The possible listening of smart assistants is not a big deal to most, except when possible personal data is being shared, then the concern of confidentiality comes to centre stage.

Smart Homes and Home Health

Confidentiality and privacy are especially large concerns in the home health community. With the elderly, smart assistants have a large possibility for integration that can improve the care received by seniors at home. It can allow the patient to have more autonomy and provide easier help with technology as the smart assistants are voice activated (Suresh & Sruthi, 2015). However, smart homes are not just limited to smart assistants. Sensors and robotics are also largely used. Whether it be to detect falls, activity, and inactivity, or other accidents, there are many technologies that can make a home into a smart home and improve the care of seniors (Birchley et al., 2017). These sensors and devices used to detect the activity of the elderly can also be used to monitor the activity of babies and their caregiver so the parents can be assured the baby is being cared for properly, hence improving the health of the parents by reducing their concern and anxiety (Zimmerman et al., 2019).

Safety and Security of Smart Homes

One important consideration of smart homes is how safe and secure they are. The safety of the tenants is of critical importance. Smart homes have the ability to save lives with their new technology. The ability for smart homes to notify emergency services in the case of a home emergency plays a critical part in the safety of the home. With emergencies such as gas and water leaks and carbon monoxide leaks, the smart home can adapt or the user can remotely turn off different systems to minimise the damage as well as notifying emergency services can save lives (Sovacool & Furszyfer Del Rio, 2020).

The smart home technology can also be useful in monitoring the activity in the house. This can be useful as any abnormal activity can save lives. Whether it be an intruder, health and safety risks to a baby in the house, or a potential fall by an elderly tenant, it can allow any family member to know what is happening in their house, or a house of a loved one and ensure the safety and security of the house (Zhang et al., 2015). Possible forms of smart home technology to ensure the security and safety of the inhabitants come in many forms. Be it in surveillance cameras, motion detectors, or sensors built into different appliances to inform of gas, water, or carbon monoxide leaks, and even door locks, these methods are the most common to ensure safety and security of the tenants within a smart home (Zimmerman et al., 2019).

Smart Security Appliances

Smart security cameras and smart doorbells are becoming very common today to ensure the security of a smart home. The smart security camera connects to the smartphone and allows for the tenant to monitor their home when away. They can set up motion detection alerts so that they can be notified by any movement in the camera's field of view. Some outdoor security cameras like the Amazon Blink allow for easy communication so that the user can speak with a person in view of the security camera. The smart doorbells act similarly but are just for the front door so the tenant can answer the door from anywhere (Amazon, n.d.).

One other equally important security measure is a lock. Now, smart lock technology is becoming very prevalent. With features like fingerprint touch or remote door unlocking and locking through a smartphone, a smart home has never been more safe. The smart lock can detect when a door is closed and lock it so the tenant never leaves the house unlocked when they are not home (Eufy, n.d.).

Smart Appliances

There are other forms of smart appliances found in smart homes. The way these appliances are designed is to provide the user as much control over their home, in many ways done through connection with a smart device. These appliances come in the form of ovens, refrigerators and freezers, vacuums, televisions, thermostats, and washing and drying machines (Kang et al., 2017).

A smart oven would have sensors that can detect how well cooked the food is and using an artificial intelligence algorithm, it would adjust its temperature and time to ensure the food is cooked to perfection. The oven would also be integrated into the user's phone, so they can monitor the oven with better control (Grogan, 2012).

Many refrigerators and freezers are smart in the power saving mechanisms they have installed. They connect to the smart grid to minimise energy usage while ensuring that the food within does not spoil. They do this by periodically shutting off during energy spikes. As well as power saving, smart refrigerators are beginning to elevate the meal prep process. They can suggest what food the user should eat, when to eat a certain food, and how to prepare the food. With its integration into the user's phone, it can remind the user to check certain food in the fridge so it does not go to waste (Grogan, 2012).

Smart vacuums, such as the Roomba, are very common in households nowadays. Over two million Roombas have been sold in the United States. This smart vacuum has many unique capabilities. Firstly, it vacuums the single level surface it is on without human assistance. This is a huge time saver as it means the user does not need to spend time vacuuming floors as the Roomba runs autonomously. The only human assistance it needs is to be placed on levels other than that of its dock, and when on those levels, to be returned back so it can empty the collected dirt into the dock. Secondly, it maps the floor plan of the single level. This allows it to consistently vacuum the floor reliably without missing areas. It does this by using local IR and bump sensors that detect walls, counters, and even drops from stairs. This ensures the smart vacuum does not get broken by hitting walls or running off an edge and down a set of stairs. Lastly, it connects to the phone so the tenant can run the Roomba remotely from its dock to clean the level. The phone integration also allows the Roomba to clean multiple levels as it saves floor plans and when placed on a new level, the user can select the corresponding floor plan and run the Roomba (Tribelhorn & Dodds, 2007).

Even televisions are having large improvements in the smart home sector. The main feature of a smart tv is the ability for the television itself to connect to the internet and access online content such as Netflix, Youtube, and Disney+ (Shin et al., 2013). The arguably bigger feature of a smart television which is becoming more prominent in newer televisions is the ability to cast content from a mobile device or laptop wirelessly onto the television. One large example of this is the Chromecast by google. What first was a device that is connected to the television, is now being built into many televisions (Google, n.d.).

Smart thermostats have large applications in the smart home to help with heating and cooling. It allows the tenant to control the heating and cooling in their home remotely. It also provides the tenant with a way to schedule heating and cooling cycles based on their needs (Mysa, n.d.).

A smart washing machine has many unique features. They have sensors to detect the load weight. In turn, they can optimise water usage and minimise total wash time and water used. One other unique feature is the ability to run a self-diagnosis. When connected to Wi-Fi, the washing machine can determine what is wrong with it. This ability to self-diagnose reduces the need for the user to call a repairman to come to fix it. When the washing machine is connected to the user's phone, they can monitor the status of the wash and adjust the cycles and adjust the amount of fabric softener in the load. With a shift to integration to the smart grid, the smart washing machine users can monitor their energy usage, and shift usage to lower usage times (Grogan, 2012).

Smart Home Security Risks

Due to the nature of smart homes constantly sharing data through a command centre like a smartphone, smart homes are highly susceptible to hacking and data stealing. This risk is increased by the merging of physical and cyber applications into the home as there are now more avenues to access and steal data from a smart home. A hacked smart home could cause the tenant to lose control of their home with the hacker being able to control the home instead. A large risk of a hacked smart home is the hacker being able to look at trends in the data to deduce daily habits or personal data. Monitoring when the lights turn on and off throughout the day would allow the hacker to determine when would be an ideal time to rob the house as they could deduce when the tenants would not be home most likely. Thus, as the risk of a smart home security breach increases, the level of security of the smart home also increases to match the elevated risk (Geneiatakis et al., 2017).

Smart Lighting and Subsurfaces

Smart lighting uses smart light bulbs that can be controlled by either a phone or a smart personal assistant. The smart light bulbs are paired via Bluetooth to the command centre. These lights are able to be dimmed, turned on and turned off by these command centres. Many smart lights are even able to change their colour. The smart lights allow the user versatile and easy control over their home which improves their comfort level in their home. Some ways to personalise a smart home with smart light bulbs include setting up different combinations of lights and colours throughout the house and can be programmed to be turned on at different times of the day (Philips Hue, n.d.).

A subsurface is any surface along a wall that is not a wall, such as doors and windows. A smart subsurface means a window or door uses smart technology to be better at its task. A smart window is a window that is able to dynamically control light and energy transmitted through the window. To dynamically control indoor lighting, one method is by using materials in the window that are translucent at low heat, and opaque at high heat. This method works because on less sunny days and at night time, more sun and moon light is allowed through to help with indoor lighting. On a more sunny day, less light is allowed through to moderate the lighting indoors (Ke et al., 2019). Smart windows allow dynamic control over energy efficiency and improves the comfort inside the building. Smart windows allow for better control over the temperature and lighting within a building better than a regular window. Windows are the weak spot within a building where they will let in or out too much heat. They drastically raise the cost spent on heating and cooling the house. It is suggested that smart windows are able to save roughly 4.5% on energy bills per year (Granqvist, 2014). The way a smart window operates to reduce energy is by using the outdoor temperature to modulate the indoor temperature. If heating is desired, then the smart window will allow solar irradiation through. The solar radiation will assist in home heating. If cooling is desired, then solar irradiation being sent through the window will be blocked, reducing the heat in the home (Ke et al., 2019). The energy usage of the smart windows must consider user satisfaction as the primary goal. They are dependent on their control strategies and should consider the location of users in relation to the electrochromic smart window (Granqvist, 2014).

Smart Home Technology Interactions

After reviewing the aspects, appliances, and devices used within a smart home and their purposes, the interactions between different integrated smart devices starts with the command centre. This is where most of the smart devices connect to and allow for remote control of appliances within the smart home. This command centre is typically a smartphone, however it has optional input in the form of smart personal assistants like the Amazon Echo or the Google Home (Mulcahy et al., 2019). This command centre allows for remote control and monitoring of different appliances from ovens to refrigerators to smart lights which provides the user control and more comfort in their home (Grogan, 2012). From there, many appliances integrate with the smart grid to save money and be energy efficient (Nepveu & Diaz, 2010). As a result the smart home achieves its goal which is to improve the comfort, entertainment, security and management of the tenant (Harper, 2003).

Conclusion

The new technology in these smart appliances, in the forms of artificial intelligence, machine learning, high-tech sensors, and robotics, turn these simple homes into smart homes powered by smart high technology devices and are very influential in improving the lives of the homeowners. Yes, there are some privacy and confidentiality concerns, especially when working with smart personal assistants, however, when looking at the pros versus the cons, it is clear that the positive impact of the smart homes on the resident greatly outweighs any concerns that residents living with smart appliances, assistants, and other technology may have about it.

References

Amazon.ca. (n.d.). Blink. Retrieved December 31, 2022, from https://www.amazon.ca/stores/page/C7F6AE4F-1503-4C7F-81BD-B9C961BE9035?maas-=maas_adg_api_8754005000801_macro_1_1&ref_=aa_maas&aa_campaignid=15516143272&aa_adgroupid=131438806552&aa_cre-ativeid=ad-605961463857_kwd-11358250047_dev-c_ext-&gclid=Cj0KCQiAtbqdBhDvARIsAGYnXBOvX2-bro6N-rCeqQNFD38JyWL0_4fO5APif7FRpiR4d9HLzJoLzgVIaAm-ROEALw_wcB

Birchley, G., Huxtable, R., Murtagh, M., ter Meulen, R., Flach, P., & Gooberman-Hill, R. (2017). Smart Homes, private homes? an empirical study of technology researchers' perceptions of ethical issues in developing SMART-Home Health Technologies. BMC Medical Ethics, 18(1). https://doi.org/10.1186/s12910-017-0183-z

Edu, J. S., Such, J. M., & Suarez-Tangil, G. (2021). Smart Home Personal Assistants: A Security and Privacy Review. ACM Computing Surveys, 53(6), 1–36. https://doi.org/10.1145/3412383

Eufy. (n.d.). Smart lock touch & wi-fi□black□. eufy. Retrieved December 31, 2022, from https://us.eufy.com/products/t8520

Geneiatakis, D., Kounelis, I., Neisse, R., Nai-Fovino, I., Steri, G., & Baldini, G. (2017). Security and privacy issues for an IOT based Smart Home. 2017 40th International Convention on Information and Communication Technology, Electronics and Microelectronics (MIPRO). https://doi.org/10.23919/mipro.2017.7973622

Google. (n.d.). Chromecast built-in - TV. Google. Retrieved December 30, 2022, from https://www.google.com/chromecast/built-in/tv/

Granqvist, C. G. (2014). Electrochromics for smart windows: Oxide-based thin films and devices. Thin Solid Films, 564, 1–38. https://doi.org/10.1016/j.tsf.2014.02.002

Grogan, A. (2012). Smart appliances. Engineering & Technology, 7(6), 44. https://doi.org/10.1049/et.2012.0603

Guo, X., Shen, Z., Zhang, Y., & Wu, T. (2019). Review on the application of Artificial Intelligence in smart homes. Smart Cities, 2(3), 402–420. https://doi.org/10.3390/smartcities2030025

Harper, R. (2003). Inside the smart home. Springer.

Kang, W. M., Moon, S. Y., & Park, J. H. (2017). An enhanced security framework for home appliances in Smart Home. Human-Centric Computing and Information Sciences, 7(1). https://doi.org/10.1186/s13673-017-0087-4

Ke, Y., Chen, J., Lin, G., Wang, S., Zhou, Y., Yin, J., Lee, P. S., & Long, Y. (2019). Smart Windows: Electro, Thermo, Mechano, Photochromics, and Beyond. Advanced Energy Materials, 9(39), 1902066–n/a. https://doi.org/10.1002/aenm.201902066

Koteluk, O., Wartecki, A., Mazurek, S., Kołodziejczak, I., & Mackiewicz, A. (2021). How do machines learn? artificial intelligence as a new era in medicine. Journal of Personalized Medicine, 11(1), 32. https://doi.org/10.3390/jpm11010032

Mulcahy, R., Letheren, K., McAndrew, R., Glavas, C., & Russell-Bennett, R. (2019). Are households ready to engage with smart home technology? Journal of Marketing Management, 35(15-16), 1370–1400. https://doi.org/10.1080/0267257x.2019.1680568

Mysa. (n.d.). Mysa smart thermostat for baseboard heaters: Electric heat. Mysa Smart Thermostat for Baseboard Heaters | Electric Heat. Retrieved December 30, 2022, from https://shop.getmysa.com/products/mysa-baseboard

Nepveu, J., & Diaz, N. M. (2010). What is the smart grid and why should we care? Clearinghouse Review, 44(5-6), 302–.

Oliveira, L., Mitchell, V., & May, A. (2019). Smart home technology—comparing householder expectations at the point of installation with experiences 1 year later. Personal and Ubiquitous Computing, 24(5), 613–626. https://doi.org/10.1007/s00779-019-01302-4

Philips Hue EN-CA. (n.d.). Smart light bulbs. Retrieved December 30, 2022, from https://www.philips-hue.com/en-ca/products/smart-light-bulbs

Shin, D., Hwang, Y., & Choo, H. (2013). Smart TV: Are they really smart in interacting with people? understanding the interactivity of Korean Smart TV. Behaviour & Information Technology, 32(11), 1194–1195. https://doi.org/10.1080/0144929x.2013.782842

Sovacool, B. K., & Furszyfer Del Rio, D. D. (2020). Smart Home Technologies in Europe: A critical review of concepts, benefits, risks and policies. Renewable and Sustainable Energy Reviews, 120, 109663. https://doi.org/10.1016/j.rser.2019.109663

Suresh, S., & Sruthi, P. V. (2015). A review on Smart Home Technology. 2015 Online International Conference on Green Engineering and Technologies (IC-GET). https://doi.org/10.1109/get.2015.7453832

Sweeney, M., & Davis, E. (2021). Alexa, are you listening? Information Technology and Libraries, 39(4). https://doi.org/10.6017/ital.v39i4.12363

Tribelhorn, B., & Dodds, Z. (2007). Evaluating the Roomba: A low-cost, ubiquitous platform for robotics research and Education. Proceedings 2007 IEEE International Conference on Robotics and Automation. https://doi.org/10.1109/robot.2007.363179

Zhang, J., Shan, Y., & Huang, K. (2015). Isee Smart Home (ISH): Smart Video Analysis for Home Security. Neurocomputing, 149, 752–766. https://doi.org/10.1016/j.neucom.2014.08.002

Zimmermann, V., Gerber, P., Marky, K., Böck, L., & Kirchbuchner, F. (2019). Assessing users' privacy and security concerns of Smart Home Technologies. i-Com, 18(3), 197–216. https://doi.org/10.1515/icom-2019-0015

DATA COLLECTED BY SEARCH ENGINES AND SOCIAL MEDIA APPLICATIONS

By Hala Mahdi

Data Collected by Search Engines - Introduction

Search engines are an essential component of the internet, and crucial tools for navigating the masses of information available online. Search engines largely predate social media, as by 2009, 84% of all internet users had used a web search engine at least once (Castella-Roca et al., 2009). The most popular search engines (Google, Yahoo!, Bing, etc) have been continually evolving in the past three decades, however concerns relating to data collection and efforts to protect user privacy have become more prevalent after the turn of the century (Zimmer, 2008). Web search engines are notorious for their data collection, using the massive amounts of data mined to personalise the searching experience, tailoring results and advertisements to each individual user (Castella-Roca et al., 2009). A wide assortment of data is typically collected, including but not limited to IP addresses, cookies, geolocation, click-through histories, and search histories (Nininahazwe & Taylor, 2018).

A Brief Focus on Google

While Google was not the first search engine launched (a title reserved for Yahoo! in 1994), the infamous web search engine launched in 1998 currently massively dominates the industry, controlling 86% of the market (Bang et al., 2021). Google collects its profits through selling targeted advertisements through using internet cookies that carry user information from website to website. This data is then used to create a user profile for each individual user and ultimately an arsenal of targeted ads (Tene, 2008). The data collected from Google and other search engines is also notably used by security agencies such as the NSA and FBI to scan for potential national and international security threats. These agencies will easily expend billions of dollars on this type of online surveillance, taking advantage of the vast ocean of personal data collected by these search engines (Tene, 2008). All of this considered, it is clear that Google's databases for personal information are in no means secure, with Privacy International (a leading advocate for human rights) releasing a consultation report that ranked Google's privacy policies as the worst out of over 20 Internet service providers (Privacy International, 2007). One prominent reason for this is that Google fails to follow otherwise generally accepted privacy practices, namely the international OECD Privacy Guidelines (Privacy International, 2007).

The continued widespread use of Google is a paradox in of itself, well described by one user as him "feeling a 'weird tension' about his love of Google's products and his fear about its omnipresence in his life" (Zimmer, 2008). This is similarly demonstrated in a 2012 survey conducted by Pew Research Center on search engine use (Purcell et al., 2012). Three quarters of users reported that they would "not be okay" with the collection of their data for personalised search results, but at the same time users were using search engines more frequently than they had been in the past. In fact, 54% of respondents reported using search engines at least once or more per day in 2012, compared to 35% in 2004 (Purcell et al., 2012). This shows that web search engine users are largely aware and disapproving of the methods behind the targeted advertising and search results that they encounter during their use of the search engines, but that this ultimately is not a deterrent for most.

An Alternative Search Engine for Increased Privacy - The Case of DuckDuckGo

While the most popular search engines (Google, Yahoo, Bing, etc) as discussed above are notorious for questionable privacy policies and Big Data collection, there are some promising alternatives. A well known search engine is DuckDuckGo, founded in 2008 and claims to emphasise user privacy with features such as private searching, tracker blocking, and site encryption ("About DuckDuckGo", n.d.). While this does mean that users will not see targeted advertisements that are as accurate as Google's, it is clear from its growing success that search privacy is greatly valued amongst internet users (Parsania, 2016). In fact, DuckDuckGo has gone from having an annual total of around 16 million search queries in 2010 to an annual rate of around 35 billion search queries in 2021, showing astounding growth and the increasing value of data privacy amongst users (Saravanos et al., 2022). Using DuckDuckGo is quite convenient, as it offers all of the same features as popular engines and can be easily added as an add-on to the user's preferred browser (Google Chrome, Mozilla Firefox, etc) (Mallon, 2017). DuckDuckGo also has a separate blog at www.spreadprivacy.com, where they provide advice on reducing online footprints through privacy crash courses, as well as tips and tricks for different devices ("Privacy Newsletter...", n.d.).

Data Collected by Search Engines - Conclusion

User privacy is an issue that has been steadily increasing in popularity and concern over the past two decades, with more and more users valuing the protection of their personal data over the convenience of targeted advertisements and accurate searches (Purcell et al., 2012). While the current state of user privacy with popular search engines, namely Google, does not seem promising , it is important to note that other options exist. Google is notorious for its widespread data collection and sharing across its different platforms and outside corporations and agencies, and as such users should be vigilant of their activity on the search engine (Privacy International, 2007). However, alternative up-and-coming search engines that prioritise user privacy such as DuckDuckGo are rapidly growing in popularity and should be seriously considered as options for internet searching. These search engines are typically free-for-use and offer the same, if not more, features that the Google search engine does, all while providing convenient ways to incorporate them into your existing browser of choice (Mallon, 2017).

Data Collected By Social Media - Introduction

Online social networks such as Facebook, Instagram, or Twitter, are typically owned by a singular business that typically also controls data collection on that network, making them locally centralized services (Bahri et al., 2018). It is no secret that these networks profit largely off of targeted and retargeted marketing and advertising in return for the free use of their services (Scott, 2015). These strategies depend on extensive data collection from users to learn as much as possible about them:

their habits, spending patterns, locations, tastes, and even their states of mind at any given moment (Bahri et al., 2018).

Process and Types of Data Collection from Online Social Networks

Online social network data collection differs greatly from traditional methods of data collection. Surveys, experiments, and content analysis are all types of traditional data collection methods that involve the researchers actively playing a role in the collection and potentially alter the results in the process (Grant-Muller et al., 2015). Social media harvesting involves the collection of data unobtrusively and automatically through computer programs on a global scale (Grant-Muller et al., 2015). Collection of Big Data from social media (including but not limited to social media networks, blogs, and microblogs), otherwise known as social media harvesting, is the fourth primary method of data collection in social sciences (Yang, 2018). Practically all user activity on online social networks is tracked and collected through social media harvesting, including but not limited to images, blogs, tweets, point of interest or location data, and searches (Yang, 2018).

There are a few types of data collection by online social networks, as concisely outlined in a paper by Pelau et al. The first is consumer driven data collection, where the consumer is either aware of the collection and/or introduces the data themselves (inputting birthdates, full names, etc.), or where the consumer is unaware of the collection (i.e downloading an application with access to device data) (Pelau et al,., 2019). The second is technology driven data, where information is automatically collected, again with either permitted access (i.e HTTP cookies), or without permitted access (i.e active location on mobile devices without permission) (Pelau et al., 2019). A real world example of technology driven data collection without explicit permitted access is when Facebook launched the

Messenger application in 2011, and the default settings were to collect and display geolocation information in conversations until 2015 (Baccarella et al., 2018). Users were seemingly unable to retract already-sent locations and were able to view the precise locations of anyone they chatted with (Baccarella et al., 2018). Last is business driven data collection, which is split into data analysis by human third parties (i.e targeted advertising based on social media profiles), and data analysis by artificial intelligence (i.e algorithm-based recommendations) (Pelau et al., 2019).

The User Perspective

From the user perspective, many online social network users are aware of their personal data being collected and are understandably concerned. In fact, a survey by the Pew Research Center reported that the majority of adults "feel that their privacy is being challenged along such core dimensions...", citing security of personal information and confidentiality as major worries (Madden., 2014). However, this has not stopped individuals from using online social networks, with the University of Maine reporting that in 2021, 4.48 billion people were using online social networks worldwide (University of Maine., 2021). This dichotomy of information privacy concern and actual behaviour is often referred to as the privacy paradox (Kokolakis, 2017). Several studies have reported that online privacy concerts and posting behaviour were not correlated, with users not necessarily regulating levels of self-disclosure and activity visibility despite self-reporting concerns regarding their privacy (Hughes-Roberts, 2013; Reynolds et al., 2011; Tufekci, 2008).

The Legality and Ethics of Social Media Data Collection - A Brief Analysis of the Terms of Service

Considering the legality and ethics of this data collection, it is important to gather some context on the Terms of Service or Terms of Conditions (TOS/TOC) of these social media applications. There is a lack of clear norms revolving around the issue of breaching the TOS for the purpose of data collection, regardless of what the purpose of the data is for (Metcalf & Crawford, 2016). However, it is entirely possible that the companies that collect Big Data from social media are not entirely violating the TOS, which is an issue of a greater magnitude. In fact, an analysis of current data collection provisions in social media TOS reveals that although these provisions do exist and are common, they are "ambiguous, inconsistent, and lack context" (Fiesler et al., 2020). Not only this, but the TOS of social media websites and applications are notoriously difficult to get through, with many studies confirming that online terms and conditions such as those are "highly complex to the point of being unreadable and in many cases practically incomprehensible" (Fiesler et al., 2020). This enables Big Data collection companies and agencies to work around loopholes and remain assured that, with the exception of massive data breaches, users will generally remain none-the-wiser of the TOS terms being violated (Fiesler et al., 2020). This does not include TOS that actually explicitly allow for data collection and/or sharing, such as that of Facebook. A recent controversy surrounding this occurred when Facebook Acquired the messaging app WhatsApp and updated its conditions to include that the platforms would automatically link datasets, inevitably to be used for marketing purposes (Flynn., 2021).

Decentralised Online Social Networks - A Potential Solution

Going back to online social networks being locally centralised services, this is what largely causes the serious threats to user privacy. Currently, a few centralised groups have access to an uncontrolled collection of data from billions of individuals worldwide (Bahri et al., 2018). A solution for this has been introduced in the new field of research surrounding decentralised online social networks (Bahri et al., 2018). It is generally agreed upon that if decentralisation is executed correctly, then virtually all of the major privacy concerns with the current locally centralised model should be resolved. There are two leading approaches to decentralising online social networks: a more moderate approach of creating a system of multiple independent federated servers providing the same online social network functionality that users are able to choose from and then switch between freely, or an extreme approach of creating direct peer-to-peer networks of personal devices (phones, laptops, tablets, etc) with direct interactions between them (Bahri et al., 2018; Buchegger et al., 2009, Shakimov et al., 2011). However, the field is still relatively new, and predictably comes with its own sets of technical limitations. Not only that, but decentralised online social networks actually introduced a new privacy concern, if the collection and control of data was previously controlled by a single centralised entity, now it falls upon the individuals in the decentralised system to complete those tasks (Bahri et al., 2018). This includes data retrieval and backup, content storage and management, and essentially deciding who gets to upload what content and who gets to see it (De Salve et al., 2022). While there are solutions currently being proposed and implemented for this, the current literature still lacks a systemization of decentralised online social networks that would allow for a universal approach (Di Pietro., 2022).

Beneficial Applications of Data Collected by Social Media Applications

On the other hand, it is also important to note some of the beneficial applications of locally centralised infrastructures for online social networks. The two primary applications that will be discussed in this chapter are health and epidemiological research, and crisis response and management.

In terms of health, Big Data collected through social media is most often applied towards epidemiological research and surveillance activities (Mayer et al., 2016). While of course, data collected through online social networks is not as accurate or precise as data collected through actual clinical or epidemiological studies, the sheer amount of it provides a much larger database than any electronic health network could (Mayer et al., 2016). In a literature review of over 100 epidemiological studies that utilised digital data, 31% used social media, most of which was obtained from tweets and blog posts (Park et al., 2018). An example of this is a study by Chary et al., where they were able to accurately estimate the geographic distribution of the misuse of prescription opioids in the United States based on the geographic location of tweets that contained at least one keyword related to opioid use (Chary et al., 2017). Another fascinating study using data from social media for health research is one conducted by Park et al. in 2019, who focused on collecting data from Pinterest on pins relating to skin cancer (Park et al., 2019). They deduced that a combination of visual characteristics and information richness resulted in the best user engagement, and were able to create suggestions for creating effective prevention messages for circulation on Pinterest (Park et al., 2019).

Additionally, data collected from social media has also proven to be an effective tool for emergency management teams and systems in recent years. A prime example of this is the Slándáil project headed by Ireland, the UK, Italy, and Germany that created a social media monitor that collects all messages from social media sources that are tagged as being from the geolocation of the crisis or disaster ("Security System...", n.d.). Then, they used learning techniques to organise the social media data, including natural language processing for identifying relevant keywords and phrases, as well as image recognition and analysis (hayes et al., 2018; Musaccho et al., 2017). In a case study conducted by Kelly et al., they utilised this system in a demonstration using Twitter data from the December 20th of 2015 to January 2nd of 2016 in Ireland, when a series of severe storms and floods occurred (Kelly et al., 2017). They demonstrated that the temporal component as well as the location of the Twitter messages collected and analysed can be used to identify conversations about the flooding events in Ireland during that time period (Kelly et al., 2017). This timely information could then be given for emergency management teams to aid in their situational awareness of the crises and ultimately support their real-time decision making (Kelly et al., 2017).

Social Media Data Collection - Conclusion

Online social networks and social media applications are a relatively new development in the 21st century, and therefore predictably come with their fair share of both drawbacks and benefits. In this chapter, a description of the processes and types of data collection by these online social networks was given, alongside a brief overview of user attitudes and behaviours with regards to their privacy and social media. Additionally, the ethics and legalities of data collection from these networks as well as some alternatives to the current locally centralised architecture of the network were described. Finally, some benefits of data collection by online social networks include data used for health and epidemiological research, as well as for natural disaster response and management.

References

A Race to the Bottom – Privacy Ranking of Internet Service Companies. (2007). [Consultation Report]. Privacy International. https://privacyinternational.org/sites/default/files/2017-12/A_Race_Bottom.pdf

About DuckDuckGo. (n.d.). Retrieved December 30, 2022, from https://duckduckgo.com/about

Baccarella, C. V., Wagner, T. F., Kietzmann, J. H., & McCarthy, I. P. (2018). Social media? It's serious! Understanding the dark side of social media. European Management Journal, 36(4), 431–438. https://doi.org/10.1016/j.emj.2018.07.002

Bahri, L., Carminati, B., & Ferrari, E. (2018). Decentralized privacy preserving services for Online Social Networks. Online Social Networks and Media, 6, 18–25. https://doi.org/10.1016/j.osnem.2018.02.001

Bang, J., Buschman, A. C., Gates, J., Kuc, R. D., & Navarro, V. (2021). Panic! At The Search Engine. Communication Complications.

Buchegger, S., Schiöberg, D., Vu, L.-H., & Datta, A. (2009). PeerSoN: P2P social networking: early experiences and insights. Proceedings of the Second ACM EuroSys Workshop on Social Network Systems - SNS '09, 46–52. https://doi.org/10.1145/1578002.1578010

Castellà-Roca, J., Viejo, A., & Herrera-Joancomartí, J. (2009). Preserving user's privacy in web search engines. Computer Communications, 32(13–14), 1541–1551. https://doi.org/10.1016/j.comcom.2009.05.009

Chary, M., Genes, N., Giraud-Carrier, C., Hanson, C., Nelson, L. S., & Manini, A. F. (2017). Epidemiology from Tweets: Estimating Misuse of Prescription Opioids in the USA from Social Media. Journal of Medical Toxicology, 13(4), 278–286. https://doi.org/10.1007/s13181-017-0625-5

De Salve, A., Mori, P., Ricci, L., & Di Pietro, R. (2022). Content Privacy Enforcement Models in Decentralized Online Social Networks: State of Play, Solutions, Limitations, and Future Directions (arXiv:2206.03084). arXiv. http://arxiv.org/abs/2206.03084

Di Pietro, R. (2022). Securing Content in Decentralized Online Social Networks: Solutions, Limitations, and the Road Ahead. Proceedings of the 27th ACM on Symposium on Access Control Models and Technologies, 1–2. https://doi.org/10.1145/3532105.3535041

Fiesler, C., Beard, N., & Keegan, B. C. (2020). No Robots, Spiders, or Scrapers: Legal and Ethical Regulation of Data Collection Methods in Social Media Terms of Service. Proceedings of the International AAAI Conference on Web and Social Media, 14, 187–196. https://doi.org/10.1609/icwsm.v14i1.7290

Flynn, S. (n.d.). Social Media Privacy: Legalities of Personal Data Collection – IP Osgoode. Retrieved December 29, 2022, from https://www.iposgoode.ca/2021/04/social-media-privacy-legalities-of-personal-data-collection/

Grant☐Muller, S. M., Gal☐Tzur, A., Minkov, E., Nocera, S., Kuflik, T., & Shoor, I. (2015). Enhancing transport data collection through social media sources: Methods, challenges and opportunities for textual data. IET Intelligent Transport Systems, 9(4), 407–417. https://doi.org/10.1049/iet-its.2013.0214

Hayes, P., & Kelly, S. (2018). Distributed morality, privacy, and social media in natural disaster response. Technology in Society, 54, 155–167. https://doi.org/10.1016/j.techsoc.2018.05.003

Hughes-Roberts, T. (2013). Privacy and Social Networks: Is Concern a Valid Indicator of Intention and Behaviour? 2013 International Conference on Social Computing, 909–912. https://doi.org/10.1109/SocialCom.2013.140

Kelly, S., Zhang, X., & Ahmad, K. (2017). Mining Multimodal Information on Social Media for Increased Situational Awareness. International Conference on Information Systems for Crisis Response and Management.

Kokolakis, S. (2017). Privacy attitudes and privacy behaviour: A review of current research on the privacy paradox phenomenon. Computers & Security, 64, 122–134. https://doi.org/10.1016/j.cose.2015.07.002

Madden, M. (2014, November 12). Public Perceptions of Privacy and Security in the Post-Snowden Era. Pew Research Center: Internet, Science & Tech. https://www.pewresearch.org/internet/2014/11/12/public-privacy-perceptions/

Mallon, M. (2017). Digital Privacy and Security. Public Services Quarterly, 13(4), 260–267. https://doi.org/10.1080/15228959.2017.1375884

Mayer, M. A., Fernández-Luque, L., & Leis, A. (2016). Big Data For Health Through Social Media. In Participatory Health Through Social Media (pp. 67–82). Elsevier. https://doi.org/10.1016/B978-0-12-809269-9.00005-0

Metcalf, J., & Crawford, K. (2016). Where are human subjects in Big Data research? The emerging ethics divide. Big Data & Society, 3(1), 205395171665021. https://doi.org/10.1177/2053951716650211

Musaccho, M.T. & Panizzon, R. (2017). Localising or globalising? Multilingualism and lingua franca in the management of emergencies from natural disasters. University of Padova. Retrieved from http://www.cultusjournal.com/files/Archives/Musacchio_Panizzon.pdf

Park, H.-A., Jung, H., On, J., Park, S. K., & Kang, H. (2018). Digital Epidemiology: Use of Digital Data Collected for Non-epidemiological Purposes in Epidemiological Studies. Healthcare Informatics Research, 24(4), 253. https://doi.org/10.4258/hir.2018.24.4.253

Park, S.-E., Tang, L., Bie, B., & Zhi, D. (2019). All pins are not created equal: Communicating skin cancer visually on Pinterest. Translational Behavioral Medicine, 9(2), 336–346. https://doi.org/10.1093/tbm/iby044

Parsania, V. S., Kalyani, F., & Kamani, K. (2016). A comparative analysis: DuckDuckGo vs. Google search engine. GRD Journals-Global Research and Development Journal for Engineering, 2(1), 12-17.

Pelau, C., Stanescu, M., & Serban, D. (2019). Big-Data and Consumer Profiles – The hidden traps of data collection on social media networks. Proceedings of the International Conference on Business Excellence, 13(1), 1070–1078. https://doi.org/10.2478/picbe-2019-0093

Privacy and Social Networks: Is Concern a Valid Indicator of Intention and Behaviour? | IEEE Conference Publication | IEEE Xplore. (n.d.). Retrieved December 29, 2022, from https://ieeexplore.ieee.org/abstract/document/6693437/authors#authors

Privacy Newsletter from DuckDuckGo. (n.d.). Spread Privacy. Retrieved December 30, 2022, from https://spreadprivacy.com/tag/privacy-newsletter/

Purcell, K., Rainie, L., & Brenner, J. (2012). Search engine use 2012.

Reynolds, B., Venkatanathan, J., Gonçalves, J., & Kostakos, V. (2011). Sharing Ephemeral Information in Online Social Networks: Privacy Perceptions and Behaviours. In P. Campos, N. Graham, J. Jorge, N. Nunes, P. Palanque, & M. Winckler (Eds.), Human-Computer Interaction – INTERACT 2011 (Vol. 6948, pp. 204–215). Springer Berlin Heidelberg. https://doi.org/10.1007/978-3-642-23765-2_14

Saravanos, A., Zervoudakis, S., Zheng, D., Nanda, A., Shaheen, G., Hornat, C., ... & Ang, W. (2022). Reputation, Risk, and Trust on User Adoption of Internet Search Engines: The Case of DuckDuckGo. In International Conference on Human-Computer Interaction (pp. 683-691). Springer, Cham.

Scott, D. M. (2015). The new rules of marketing & PR: How to use social media, online video, mobile applications, blogs, news releases, and viral marketing to reach buyers directly (Fifth edition). John Wiley & Sons, Inc.

Security System for language and image analysis | SLANDAIL Project | Fact Sheet | FP7 | CORDIS | European Commission. (n.d.). Cordis EU Research Results. Retrieved December 29, 2022, from https://cordis.europa.eu/project/id/607691

Seigneur Nininahazwe, F., & Ernest Taylor, M. (2018). Best Practices to Protect Your Privacy Against Search Engines Data Mining – A Review. Internet of Things and Cloud Computing, 6(3), 56. https://doi.org/10.11648/j.iotcc.20180603.11

Shakimov, A., Lim, H., Caceres, R., Cox, L. P., Li, K., Dongtao Liu, & Varshavsky, A. (2011). Vis-à-Vis: Privacy-preserving online social networking via Virtual Individual Servers. 2011 Third International Conference on Communication Systems and Networks (COMSNETS 2011), 1–10. https://doi.org/10.1109/COMSNETS.2011.5716497

Social Media Statistics Details—Undiscovered Maine—University of Maine. (n.d.). Undiscovered Maine. Retrieved December 29, 2022, from https://umaine.edu/undiscoveredmaine/small-business/resources/marketing-for-small-business/social-media-tools/social-media-statistics-details/

Tufekci, Z. (2008). Can You See Me Now? Audience and Disclosure Regulation in Online Social Network Sites. Bulletin of Science, Technology & Society, 28(1), 20–36. https://doi.org/10.1177/0270467607311484

Tene, O. (2008). What google knows: Privacy and internet search engines. Utah L. Rev., 1433.

https://link.springer.com/referenceworkentry/10.1007/978-1-4614-8265-9_80630

Yang, Y. (2018). Social Media Harvesting. In L. Liu & M. T. Özsu (Eds.), Encyclopedia of Database Systems (pp. 3533–3537). Springer New York. https://doi.org/10.1007/978-1-4614-8265-9_80630

Zimmer, M. (2008). Privacy on Planet Google: Using the Theory of "Contextual Integrity" to Clarify the Privacy Threats of Google's Quest for the Perfect Search Engine. 3(1). http://digitalcommons.law.umaryland.edu/jbtl/vol3/iss1/8

CONCLUSION

This collection of essays has focused on the topic of data privacy in a digital age, an increasingly pressing issue as we are continually faced with unprecedented technological developments. Data privacy as we have defined it is the protection of data from unauthorised collection, use, or disclosure, and is accordingly essential for the protection of personally identifiable information (PII) from corporations, agencies, and other third parties. The details of what constitutes PII and the laws related to it were discussed, highlighting the importance of privacy laws in the protection of individuals' financial and physical safety. The field of AI is one that is still relatively new and as such has been littered with examples of unethical uses and ambiguous responsibility when it comes to data privacy and using AI to collect and analyze personal data. There have also been several significant privacy breaches in recent years, an example that was discussed in this work being that of Cambridge Analytica and Facebook, where the political consulting firm obtained data from 87 million Facebook users to allegedly influence the 2018 US presidential election. Another aspect of personal privacy discussed in this work is the practice of facial scanning that is only increasing in prevalence. An example of this mentioned is Meta, Facebook and Instagram's parent company, that claims to use facial screening to ensure their users are not under the age of 18. The issues of data collected by search engines and social media were also accordingly discussed, with search engines such as Google and social media apps such as Instagram and Twitter being notorious for Big Data collection and dissemination to marketing and government agencies.

Further, other, less obvious, avenues for personal privacy collection and breaches were also discussed including those in the aviation industry, CCTV surveillance, as well as smart home technology. The aviation industry is particularly weak to privacy abuses, considering the reliance on personal identification information to verify passenger identity. Some mentioned methods of strengthening identification efforts while also increasing privacy protection include implementing biometric screening, relying on methods such as facial or fingerprint recognition. CCTV surveillance is often a double edged sword, with its benefits including real-time personal security and crime surveillance and evidence collection, while its potential harms including its abuse leading to footage gathered for blackmail use or voyeurism. Lastly, smart home technology in the form of AI, machine learning, and robotics has been able to turn simple homes into impressive technologically advanced smart homes. The benefits of this are clear and tempting, but the drawbacks were also discussed, with concerns regarding privacy issues in relation to smart personal assistants being particularly of note.

Due to breaches like those aforementioned and the recent increase in cybercrime, phishing scams and illegal mass dissemination of PII, the importance of anonymity and partaking in best practices for consumers were additionally highlighted. A few options for maintaining a semblance of anonymity while online include using encrypted messaging apps, storage, and browsers that prioritise user privacy, as well as using a VPN to hide user web traffic information. Additional best practices to maintain while online include the use of complex passwords and two factor authentication, as well as being vigilant and aware of possible phishing schemes. Another promising avenue for privacy protection is the recent mass use of biometrics for smartphone protection, considering biological traits such as fingerprints are much harder to steal or forge than PINs or physical cards/locks.

www.ingramcontent.com/pod-product-compliance
Lightning Source LLC
Chambersburg PA
CBHW070353200326
41518CB00012B/2225